A GUIDE TO THE HAUNTED QUEEN MARY

Ghostly apparitions, psychic phenomena and
paranormal activity aboard the world famous luxury liner

Written by

**Robert Wlodarski, Anne Nathan-Wlodarski
and Richard Senate**

Dedicated to:

ALL VISITORS
both seen and unseen
who have, or continue to grace the decks
of the Queen Mary...

May we *all* someday rest in peace!

Happy HAUNTING from ghost to coast.

A GUIDE TO THE HAUNTED QUEEN MARY

Ghostly apparitions, psychic phenomena and paranormal activity aboard the world famous luxury liner

Published by:

G-HOST PUBLISHING
8701 Lava Place
West Hills, California 91304-2126
Phone/Fax (818) 340-6676

Other Books Available through G-Host Publishing;

Haunted Catalina ($11.95)
Haunted Alamo   ($11.95)

The stories appearing in this book are based on factual accounts of everyday people who have either worked on the **Queen Mary**, been passengers, or visited the ship over the years. Carlo Giovetti's seance originally appeared in *The Haunted Southland,* by Richard Senate. The authors will be pleased to hear from our readers about their paranormal experiences aboard the **Queen Mary**, so that the most interesting of these may be included in future editions.

The authors take no responsibility for the veracity of each story. We have attempted to detail the encounters described in this book as accurately as possible. Although the publishers have made every effort to ensure that the information was correct at the time the book went to press, they do not assume, and hereby disclaim any liability to any party for any loss, damage or injury caused by information contained in this book. Furthermore, the publishers disclaim any liability resulting from the use of this book.

First Printing, 1995 - First Edition
Second Printing, 1996 - First Edition
Third Printing, 1997 - First Edition

Library of Congress Catalog Card Number: 95-78479
ISBN 0-9649088-0-8 Softcover

All photographs are provided courtesy of the RMS Foundation, Queen Mary Archives.

COVER DESIGN by Jennifer Prager.

Printed in the United States by M & M Quality Printing, Calabasas, California.

ACKNOWLEDGMENTS

*It is wonderful that five thousand years have elapsed
since the creation of the world, and still it is undecided
whether or not there has ever been an instance of the
spirit of any person appearing after death. All argument
is against it, but all belief is for it.*

Samuel Johnson - Boswell's Life (1778)

Too often during the course of any endeavor, the end product obscures the fact that a tremendous amount of time and energy was necessary to achieve it. Such was the case with this book, and the stories contained within. A number of individuals from this dimension, as well as those from "the other side," contributed their time, energy and commitment to making this a reality. To all these souls, we are truly grateful!

We would like to express our gratitude to those, whose belief, assistance and dedication made this book on the afterlife a reality in this life. That this book has found a place in the illustrious history of the **RMS Queen Mary**, represents a testament to the living as well as to those who have passed on, but choose to remain on board.

Foremost, we would like to thank *Matthew* and *Henrietta Wlodarski* for their help in publishing the second printing of this book; to *Mr. Joseph Prevratil*, President of the RMS Foundation, Inc., for his initial belief that this book would be a lasting contribution to the legacy of the *Queen Mary*; to *Ron Smith*, Exhibits Coordinator and Archivist, for his tireless support in obtaining valuable archival photographs, constructive comments, and ensuring the historical accuracy of the book; and to *Craig Post* and *Eric Prevratil* for their assistance.

We are indebted to *Jane Gilbert*, our proof-reader, for her valuable input.

We would also like to acknowledge the creative input provided by *Jennifer Prager* represented in the cover artwork.

A final note of thanks to *Michael Massoud* of M&M Printing of Calabasas, for his help in the printing of this book.

And last, but certainly not least, we would like to thank those along the way who listened and believed, including: *Debbie Christenson Senate, Richard Niederberg* and our familes and friends.

ABOUT THE AUTHORS

ROBERT WLODARSKI

Born in Los Angeles, California, Wlodarski has a broad-based educational background with an A.A. in Business/Accounting from Fullerton College, B.A.'s in History and Anthropology, and an M.A. in Anthropology from California State University, Northridge.

The President of the *Historical, Environmental, Archaeological, Research, Team* (H.E.A.R.T.) since 1978, Wlodarski has managed and administered over 370 archaeological and historical projects for various Federal, State, County, City and private sector agencies and companies. He has been a staff archaeologist for the UCLA Archaeological Survey, and California State University Northridge Center for Public Archaeology from 1973-1980. He was the Archaeological Project Leader for the California Department of Transportation from 1984-1986.

Mr. Wlodarski, the President of *Mayan Moon Productions,* is currently co-developing two syndicated television series entitled *Hauntings,* and *The Ghost Club. Wlodarski* has authored, and co-authored over 20 articles for journals, quarterlies and magazines throughout California and the Southwest. He has co-authored seven screenplays: *The Crawling Eye, Cities of Stone, The Cool Change, Illusion, No Innocents, Ghost Glass,* and *The Palace of Unknown Kings;* and has served as Technical Consultant on *Catalina: A Treasure from The Past* for Ironwood Productions. Additionally, Wlodarski has co-authored *A Guide To The Haunted Queen Mary.*

ANNE NATHAN-WLODARSKI

Born in Texas, Mrs. Nathan-Wlodarski, a registered art therapist, received her M.A. in Behavioral Psychology from the University of Houston. She has published several articles including a chapter in *California Art Therapy Trends.* She is an exhibiting artist, and the President and Founder of HEARTWORLD Arts Center for Children, a non-profit organization for abused, disabled and disadvantaged children and youths.

Mrs. Nathan-Wlodarski served as an Education Outreach Coordinator and Gallery Assistant for the City of Los Angeles' Artspace Gallery from 1989-1993. She has been featured in the media for her work with children and the arts. She was honored as a *Sunday Woman,* by the

Daily News; and was a J.C. Penney Golden Rule Award nominee. She is Vice-President of *Mayan Moon Productions;* and has co-authored six screenplays: *The Crawling Eye, Cities of Stone, The Cool Change, Illusion, No Innocents,* and *Ghost Glass.* Nathan-Wlodarski is currently co-developing two syndicated television series entitled *Hauntings* and *The Ghost Club,* and has co-authored the book *A Guide To The Haunted Queen Mary.*

RICHARD SENATE

Born in Los Angeles, Senate has been a life-long resident of Ventura County, California, earning an Associate of Arts Degree from Ventura Community College; a Bachelor's Degree in History from Long Beach State University; and performed post-graduate work in Archaeology at the University of California, Santa Barbara. Mr. Senate has worked in the Ventura County Library system; at the Albinger Archaeological Museum since 1982; as a part-time instructor at Ventura College since 1979; at the Olivas Adobe Historic Park since 1988; and conducts Cultural/Historic Tours for the City of Ventura and administers to the City's historic resources since 1993.

Mr. Senate has authored books on history, folklore and the paranormal: *De Anza Trek Costumes Study (1976); Ghosts of the Haunted Coast* (1986); *13 Hollywood Haunts* (1991); *Haunted Ventura* (1993); *Terror Tales* (1993); and, The *Haunted Southland* (1994). He also: Lectures on paranormal activity at Pierce College and Ventura Community College; conducts phantom and folklore tours throughout the southland; has appeared on talk shows and specials: *Eye on Hollywood, Good Morning, San Francisco, The Merv Griffin Show, You Bet Your Life, Sightings, Haunted Hollywood* for HBO, *The Search for Haunted Houses* for Fox; writes a weekly column for the Ventura County and Coast Reporter Newspaper *"The Psychic World"* ; is a guest columnist for the *Ventura County Star* ; has been featured in magazines as a paranormal investigator (*Fate, PSI Review, Ghosttrackers*); and is currently developing a syndicated television show, *Hauntings.*

Millions of spiritual creatures walk the earth unseen,
both when we wake, and when we sleep.
Spirits when they please, can either sex assume,
or both; so soft and uncompounded is their
essence pure, not tied or manacled with joint or
limb, nor founded on the brittle strength of bones.

JOHN MILTON

INTRODUCTION

Welcome aboard the Haunted *Queen Mary,* where you can step into the past, and easily imagine what it must have been like to sail aboard this luxurious ocean liner. Memories abound throughout the ship, conjuring up nostalgic reminiscences of a bygone era.

The skeleton of Job 534, Clyde RIver, Scotland

The lure and magic of the *Queen Mary* is as strong today as it was when Job 534 was completed. On September 26, 1934, an estimated crowd of 200,000 people braved the cold winds and intermittent rains at the John Brown & Company shipyard on the Clyde River in Scotland to hear His Majesty, King George V, and Her Majesty, Queen Mary, usher the famous ship into history.

Launching of the Queen Mary before 200,000 people

King George V addressed the large and anxious crowd with the words, "Today we come to the happy task of sending on her way, the stateliest ship now in being... alive with beauty, energy and strength." Stepping aside, her Majesty, Queen Mary, followed by saying, "I am happy to name this ship the **Queen Mary.** I wish success to her and all who sail in her." With those words, her Majesty pressed a button which launched Job 534, the **Queen Mary,** then the largest ship in the world, into history. However, the most prophetic words were uttered by the psychic Mable Fortescue- Harrison, who boldly predicted that the **Queen Mary** would know its greatest fame and popularity when she never sailed another mile and never carried another paying passenger.

HISTORICAL INFORMATION

The Royal Mail Ship **Queen Mary** had a long and illustrious career. Generally speaking, her time at sea can be divided into three periods: The Early years from 1936 to 1939; The War years from 1940 to 1946; and the Post-War years from 1947 to her last voyage in 1967.

Her early years began with her maiden voyage on May 27, 1936, as the prize of the Cunard Line. She carried 1,742 passengers (708 in First Class; 631 in Second Class; 403 in Third Class); a crew of 1,186 men and women; 100 reporters; 6,124 sacks of mail, and during her maiden voyage, the BBC installed a number of microphones aboard ship to broadcast the event around the world. In addition, three telephone operators were in place to handle the 600 telephone receivers which were located in the First Class cabins, as well as on the ship's decks. The passengers had the novelty of being able to ring each other on board, as well as calling home while at sea.

The **Queen Mary** sailed to New York from England in four days and fifteen hours, receiving a tremendous welcome upon her arrival in the United States. Mayor Fiorello La Guardia greeted the ship at Pier 90 on the Hudson River along with other dignitaries and throngs of curious New Yorkers.

Shortly after the **Queen Mary's** maiden voyage, the quest for the Blue Riband was on; this distinction going to the ship with the fastest transatlantic crossing. Although the Cunard Line denied that it was interested in the competition, it was well- known in the industry that being the fastest ship had a direct effect on passenger sales, and therefore, profits.

The **Normandie** held the record, which it set on its maiden voyage in 1935. Prior to the **Normandie,** the Riband was held by the Cunard Line from 1907 to 1929, due to the efforts of the Mauretania and **Lusitania.**

From 1929-1935, the Blue Riband was held by the **Bremen**, a German liner, her sister ship the **Europa**, and the Italian liner Rex. In August 1936, the **Queen Mary** recaptured the Riband for the Cunard Line from the **Normandie,** by traveling the distance in a record three days, twenty- three hours and fifty-seven minutes, with an average speed of more than 35 miles per hour. However, the battle for fastest ship continued back and forth with the **Normandie** until August 1938, when the **Queen Mary** once again claimed the record using a new propeller to enhance its performance. The **Queen Mary** would not lose the record again for 14 years, when, in 1952, the **SS United States,** a lighter ship with technological advancements, claimed the prize.

Life on board the ship for First Class passengers was a slice of heaven, as they were afforded every conceivable luxury and convenience. The crew and staff were highly trained to cater to the needs of everyone on board. The chefs were experts in their field, hired from some of the finest restaurants in the world. The dining salon had the largest floor space and seating capacity, and by square feet, was the largest room ever built within a ship, measuring 143 feet in length, by 118 feet in width (by cubic feet, the **Normandie** was larger). By historical standards, the three ships Christopher Columbus used to discover the New World could have been placed inside the dining room, along with the Cunard's first steamship.

Marion Davies in a First Class stateroom

Bellboys preparing for quests

Stood end to end, the ***Queen Mary*** was less than 229 feet shorter than the Empire State Building, taller than the Eiffel Tower and Washington Monument, and over twice as tall as the Pyramid of Cheops. Her height, from the keel to forward funnel, is greater than Niagara Falls. Recreation space aboard the ship is equivalent to a large football stadium. The main engines could generate a total of 160,000 horse power, which would equal the pulling-power of 40 large locomotives. The refrigeration needs of the ship would be equivalent to that of 15,000 tract homes. Her anchors equal the weight of 20 automobiles. She contains ten miles of carpeting, 700 clocks, and 600 phones. Over 500,000 pieces of glassware, china and table silver were used on board, along with 21,000 table cloths, 30,000 bedsheets, and 210,000 towels. Over 15,000 bottles of wine and spirits were stored in the wine cellar; and the interior decor was fashioned out of 56 of the world's finest and rarest woods. No wonder it was dubbed the "stateliest ship afloat."

A number of celebrities sailed aboard the ***Queen Mary,*** including: Fred Astaire, Greta Garbo, Bob Hope, Gloria Swanson, Elizabeth Taylor, Clark Gable, David Niven, Loretta Young, Marion Davies, Buster Keaton, Mary Pickford, Laurel and Hardy and many more. Prominent figures also included the Baron and Baroness de Rothschild, the Duke and Duchess of Windsor and the Vanderbilts.

Left Side: Liberace, Bob Hope, Marlene Dietrich, Fred Astaire
Right Side: Laurel and Hardy, Clark Gable, Spencer Tracy

By the time the *Queen Mary* reached New York on September 4, 1939, Hitler had invaded Poland, and World War II had begun, ushering in a new era for the ship. The British government requisitioned the *Queen Mary* for service, giving her a new coat of gray paint and converting her to a troop transport. She set sail for Australia in 1940, and, in May, boarded 5,000 Australian soldiers.

During her war years, she transported over 800,000 troops as well as passengers and refugees. She used her superior speed and maneuvering tactics as well as night-time black-outs on board to elude German U-Boats. She was well- equipped for fending off potential air strikes, carrying: Five, 40mm anti-aircraft guns, located on the bow, stern and above the bridge; twenty-four 20mm machine guns, which were located in strategic positions on the ship's upper decks; six, three-inch guns; a number of .50 and .30 caliber machine guns; and four sets of electrically fired anti-aircraft rocket launchers with twin cradles for holding 20 rockets each, which were adapted for high-angle and low-angle targets.

Additionally, special sound-detection sonar was installed to help anticipate the presence of German U-boats. Unfortunately, the noise from the ship's massive propellers made the sonar equipment all but useless. The *Queen Mary* was a "marked" ship by Adolf Hitler who offered $250,000, as well as instant hero status, to any U-Boat commander who could sink her. Her destination points included India, Australia, South America and Africa.

Prime Minister Winston Churchill made numerous trips aboard the *Queen Mary.*

Sir Winston Churchill, Walter S. Gifford and Anthony Eden

He once said, "Built for the arts of peace and to link the old world with the new, the Queens (*Mary* and *Elizabeth*) challenged the fury of Hitlerism... to defend the liberties of civilization. Vital decisions depended on their ability to continuously elude the enemy, and without their aid, the day of final victory must unquestionably have been postponed. To those who brought these two great ships into existence, the world owes a debt that will not be easy to measure."

Although the ship was fortunate enough to escape the enemy during the war, it was not exempt from tragedy. October 2, 1942, while sailing off the coast of Ireland, the *Queen Mary* accidently struck her escort cruiser the *HMS Curacoa,* literally slicing it in half. Three hundred-thirty-eight sailors out of a crew of 439, died at sea as a result of the tragic incident.

On June 20th, 1945, she arrived in New York with 14,777 American soldiers. Her tour of duty was not complete until she served for nine months as a transport carrier for American servicemen during 1946, carrying 18,900 wives and children to New York.

After being converted back to passenger service, she began her true post-war service on July 31, 1947. Gradually, with the advent of other, more improved and time-saving modes of transportation, including jet air-craft travel, she was sold. After 1,001 transatlantic crossings; three million miles at sea; transporting over two million passengers including 800,000 troops during World War II; and surviving being "marked" by Adolf Hitler, the *Queen Mary* arrived in Long Beach on December 9, 1967, after her final transatlantic voyage. At exactly 12:07 p.m., John Treasure Jones, the *Queen Mary's* last captain, announced the end of one career for the Queen of the Seas, and ushered in another—as a tourist attraction.

During the War Years, aboard the ship, politicians and world leaders made command decisions while soldiers awaited their orders below deck in cramped, stifling and claustrophobic conditions. The ship was a troop transport dodging Hitler's U-Boat commanders through the Pacific during World War II. It carried prisoners of war as well as dignitaries. They all shared the same metal frame, yet for the most part, the people on board were as different as night and day, separated not only by the decks, but by social class as well.

In its heyday, the *"Queen"* was a microcosm of society, where people from all walks of life—royalty and the working class; the young and

Crowded conditions during the War Years

the old; and people of all nationalities—sailed together. Those who worked the steaming boiler rooms, and moved about in the dark, confined themselves to the shaft alleys, barely glimpsing the light of day during their long voyages, to keep the vessel in top shape and at full speed, so those above deck could relax and enjoy the "good life."

First Class Dinning Room

Permanently docked at Pier J at the south end of the Long Beach Freeway, the **Queen Mary** is listed on the National Register of Historic Places, attesting to its unrivaled past and expert craftsmanship. The ship contains the Hotel Queen Mary with 365 restored original First Class staterooms; offers award-wining dining; contains over 85,000 square feet of multi-function space, 50,000 square feet of exhibition space; and provides tours which illuminate its illustrious history. The history of the **Queen Mary** is detailed in: *The Official Pictorial History of the Queen Mary; The Factual Story of a Great Ship R.M.S. Queen Mary Super Pictorial*; and *Gray Ghost: The R.M.S. Queen Mary at War*, available in the ship's gift shops.

Queen Mary docked at Pier J in Long Beach

A DOOR TO ANOTHER WORLD

It is no wonder, with this kind of legacy, that strange and unexplainable things continue to happen within the metal frame that holds this ship and its memories together. Sometimes it can be seen, while other times it can be heard or felt. For those who have witnessed the events, it is all too real. It is part of the oftentimes fearful unknown, a "dead zone" that sends a shiver up people's spines, makes their hair stand on end, or causes them to seek the safety of a well-lit room and find comfort in other human contact. These occurrences continue to happen with great frequency to people from all walks of life—skeptics and believers alike. As some parapsychologists suggest, where there are so many memories and emotions, there is bound to be *residual energy,* and a potential for hauntings.

With this book in hand as you take a guided or self-guided tour aboard the **Queen Mary,** you can become a part of a very special journey into the unknown; and maybe, "if the spirit is willing," you will be given a first-hand opportunity to experience a **Queen Mary** ghost.

Please be aware that when you proceed with your own ghost tour, there are several areas on the ship which are not accessible to the public. The diagrams of the ship provided in this book, illustrate areas where sightings have occurred, as well as areas which can be reached by way of a self-guided tour, and which areas can be accessed by the ship's tour.

Skeptics attribute the multitude of phenomena to natural causes, overactive imaginations and to events and circumstances which have a basis in scientific explanation. But the people who have witnessed the strange events aboard the **Queen Mary** have no doubts or illusions about what happened to them, or what they experienced. They know that something from another plane of existence, a ghost, or "energy" crossed their paths. But why?

A QUESTION OF BELIEF

The age-old questions remain: Do we survive death? and, if so, why do some choose to remain here? If we do survive, does the spirit or some form of energy remain locked in time and space, or to fulfill a specific purpose? Does a ghost represent a remnant energy from an unresolved tragedy—residue from an event that continues to repeat itself, waiting for justice or resolution, and a way to end the cycle? Are they unhappy souls looking for help—messengers or angels from another level trying to help us overcome our fear of death or save us from an impending tragedy? Or, do they willingly remain in a given space because of pleasant memories, returning to a particular place at a point in their lives when they were happy and at peace?

Perhaps this energy, or what some people call the *"spirit" or"* a *"ghost,"* represents a little of all these things: Happiness, sadness, lost souls, or angels. Maybe it is not necessary to see in order to believe—although for some it is the *only* way they will. Could it be that some of the people we see in everyday life are ghosts, quickly passing us by, only to disappear in the blink of an eye? What about those dark shadows and the cold spots which defy logic and rational explanation—and the feelings of uneasiness (or happiness) many of us have felt when we entered a place for the first time? Maybe they are ghosts!

Of all the uncertainties that exist, ghosts and the afterlife remain one of the most mysterious and intriguing. The concept defies logic, eludes scientific explanation and escapes absolute proof, yet is an integral part of our belief system. It has become an obsession for many to prove as well as disprove the concept of life after death. There has always been a deep regard and fascination with the subject that will continue long after we have left this physical plane.

Ghosts have played an important part of the history of this planet, connecting life to afterlife though myth, folklore, legend and custom. Every culture and its members have shared a personal or collective conscious experience with regard to the spirit world and ancestor worship. These experiences have ranged from love and honor, to fear and horror. Therefore, in the past, the presentation of information associated with these phenomena has been reflected in both a comedic and horrific fashion (the former possibly as a means of minimizing the frightening potential associated with the unknown).

The concept of ghosts and apparitions may have to do with the laws of the universe and gravity—the grounding of our spirit and our energy in this plane of existence; what we refer to as physical reality. The body dies, but not the spirit. It sometimes lingers, or "hangs around," so to speak. Perhaps it remains out of familiarity, or because of an addiction to a certain place; or out of repetition of old habits and patterns. As the saying goes, "old habits die hard."

Perhaps the energy we associate with a ghost cannot find its way home to a higher plane, to the light. They remain, some unhappy or confused, choosing to stay behind to watch over loved ones to deliver messages, or possibly to warn of impending disaster. Whatever the reason, that some form of energy remains, is well-documented and cannot be ignored.

THE GHOST STORIES

The stories of strange phenomena aboard the **Queen Mary** began surfacing almost immediately after the ship docked at Pier E in 1967 (later moving to Pier J in February 1971). Workers and security personnel began telling tales of ghosts roaming the decks of the ship. Whether these mysterious occurrences happened aboard the ship while it was still at sea, is mere speculation. However, there is every reason to believe that the same spiritual energy that exists now has been there all along; it simply wasn't discussed openly during that time.

Main staircase on the Queen Mary

Initially, the Wrather Corporation and Disney, early owners of the **Queen Mary,** were reluctant to admit the fact that "strange and unexplainable things" were happening aboard the ship, or to discuss the subject of ghosts. Apparently, there was some apprehension that ghosts and public relations would not mix; that the public might not accept the fact that they might have to share space with otherworldly passengers. Fearing that rumors of ghosts would spread and detract from their business by driving away potential tourists, the subject was hushed. The only stories told were related in secrecy among the staff, security guards and other personnel, who continued to witness strange events of an unknown origin.

A Haunted Corridor

Gradually, however, this mentality changed. No doubt with the advent of movies and books dealing with similar topic matter, and the dawning of the "New Age," another level of awareness was slowly fostered. The reluctance of the past gradually softened to ambivalence, followed by the realization that people were genuinely interested in, and curious about the paranormal. No doubt this coincided with the changing political and social climate around the world. People were tired of secrets being kept by politicians and the military, and were reluctant to trust the establishment and their "pat" answers.

In addition, the race for space spawned such topics as UFO sightings and abductions, crops circles and the paranormal. Finally, movies like *The Exorcist, The Entity, The Amityville Horror, Ghostbusters and Poltergeist* came face to face with *Roswell* and *Project Bluebook.* The afterlife, out-of-body experiences and ghosts were being discussed openly. Our quest for the rediscovery of the spiritual side of life was attempting to catch up with our pursuit for material satisfaction. The conservatism of this period was being replaced by the more liberal curiosity associated with looking within ourselves to find the answers to questions pertaining to our ultimate purpose in life: Why are we put here? Are we alone in the universe? What happens to us after we die? The search was on to find answers to these and other important questions, because we were facing the reality that our world was not a kind and peaceful place; that war, hatred, disease and death were all around us, and our very existence was being threatened.

For whatever reasons, paranormal investigations and psychic research were beginning to attract new followers. People seemed to be more tolerant or open to the possibilities of an afterlife. Maybe there was more to life than what met the eye. Individuals could talk about therapy sessions and channeling sessions without being completely ridiculed. One could have a personal trainer, therapist, psychic and astrologer, while discussing it all over steamed vegetables and bottled water.

An amazing shift in consciousness; a kind of spiritual renaissance was occurring. It was during this time that the owners of the *Queen Mary* began to realize that ghosts were not so bad for publicity after all. People were willing to pay to tour the corridors after midnight in search of the unexplained.

The *Queen Mary* is not the first ship to be haunted, and it certainly won't be the last. A ship that has traveled so long and so far, and has carried so many people to so many places, has countless memories stored within the rooms and corridors of its massive metal framework. There are cold spots, phantom gusts of wind, objects moving or disappearing and unexplainable electrical problems. One can hear the clanking of chains, oil drums banging and footsteps echoing in the darkness. Some people hear glasses clink and laughter ring out in the dead of night, perhaps as part of a continuing party from a bygone era.

Others who frequented the ship, or passed away on board, may not have fared so well. The good old days of parties and celebrations, also witnessed times of pain and sorrow. Who are these documented "lost souls" wandering aboard the ship? Let's find out!

JOHN PEDDER

The ship's log for Sunday, July 10, 1966 documented the following incident: At 4:00 a.m., a man was found trapped in a water-tight door.

At 4:07 a.m., the door was opened from the bridge. Within seconds, the life of 18-year-old John Pedder came to an abrupt end aboard the **Queen Mary.** Within a short time after his death, he become the most famous ghost on the ship, and has been given the nickname "The Shaft Alley Spectre." Ship's records further documented the incident by providing statements from the crew who found Pedder, crushed by mechanical door number 13 in the engine room.

According to Chief Engineer, T. Kirk, after coming on watch, he was informed by a Mr. Burgess that an accident had occurred at approximately 3:55 a.m. Fireman/ Cleaner John Pedder had been found trapped by number 13 water-tight door in starboard forward tunnel, receiving severe injuries from which he subsequently died. At the time of the accident, the vessel was in fog and all water-tight doors in the Boiler and Engine Rooms were closed on Bridge control.

When the area was examined and tested by the Chief Engineer, at 7:15 a.m, the water-tight door (horizontal type) was found to be in good working order, taking six seconds to close the maximum distance of three feet. There was no oil observed on the plates in the vicinity of the door, and the area was well-lit.

John Pedder joined the **Queen Mary** March 30th 1966. He had been engaged for three voyages as Fireman/Cleaner in the number 3 Boiler Room, and was making his 2nd voyage on bilge pumping duties in the Engine Room and Tunnels. First Junior Second Engineer, Stewart Roland Dunstan, stated for the records, that on the morning of July 10th, 1966, David Roger Cripps, Refrigerator Greaser, came to the Aft Engine Room platform and told him that someone was caught in number 13 water-tight door.

Where John Pedder died

(Photograph byRobert Wlodarski)

16

Keith Pilkington, Engineer on fog stand-by, hastened to the water-tight door after a phone call was made to the Forward Engine Room briefly explaining what happened. Upon his arrival at the scene, Dunstan stated that Mr. J. Hambly and Mr. K. Pilkington and himself released the trapped man, with Mr. Hambly keeping the door open while he and Pilkington moved the injured man away from the door. The Night Nursing Sister, called earlier by the Forward Engine Room, arrived a few minutes later and examined the injured man.

The First Senior 6th Engineer, J.H. Hambly, entered the tunnel, and immediately saw the trapped man in the door. Mr. Pilkington then held the man while Hambly opened the door. The injured man was then laid flat on the metal plates (the flooring) with as little movement as possible. Mr. Dunstan arrived and Hambly put a call through to the hospital, but they had already been informed.

Keith Pilkington, Third Junior 6th Engineer, added that since he was the first to reach the door, he could see that someone was trapped in it, with his back to him. Both the man's forearms were pinioned against his ribs by the door which shut crossways. Furthermore, the person was in a standing position with his head and shoulders through the door. Realizing the need for immediate action, Keith Pilkington operated the door release, but was unable to stop the person from falling forward through the door, where the body lay without sound or movement. Mr. Hambly took control of the water-tight door while he maneuvered the body clear of it. By this time, Mr. Dunstan had arrived, although they could all see that there was little hope for the man.

Angela Miller Jones, the Nursing Sister, was on duty when the call came. She had the Night Telephonist call Dr. Morgan, then hurried to the scene and examined John Pedder. She noted that there was no pulse palpable, and that he was cyanosed (turning blue due to lack of oxygen). There were multiple bruises over his arms and chest and he had been bleeding from both nostrils. No signs of life were present. When Dr. Morgan arrived, he ordered an intra-muscular injection of morphine, which Ms. Jones administered. The body was then transferred to the ship's hospital, and identified as John Pedder by David Cripps, the Refrigerator Greaser.

The surgeon, Dr. P.R. Morgan arrived on the scene at 4:10 a.m. Upon examination Pedder appeared to be dead, but because of the noise and vibration, and the position in which he was found, adequate examination was difficult. Pedder was given an injection of morphine and removed to the ship's hospital. On examination, no signs of life were detected. There were marks of a crushing injury on his arms, chest and pelvis, more marked on the right than left; there was some bleeding from the nose; no eye reflexes, and no external sign of injury to the head. There was no evidence of injury other than as consistent with his having been trapped in a water-tight door.

The 18-year-old Fireman/Cleaner from Skipton, Yorkshire, met his death trying to squeeze through a water-tight door that closed in less than six seconds. Why did he take such a risk on a routine drill? Was he playing a deadly game of "chicken" with another crew member for money, as some have speculated? Whatever the reason, his restless spirit is often seen or felt near the door that took his life.

Perhaps someone, someday can communicate with him to find out what really happened; why he remains trapped in Shaft Alley; and possibly set his spirit free.

WILLIAM ERIC STARK

Senior Second Officer W.E. Stark has been spotted in his quarters, as well as on deck on a number of occasions. Like John Pedder, Stark represents another victim of a senseless tragedy. The ship's records detail the cause of his accidental death.

According to the Staff Captain, Stark completed his night rounds and reported to him at 2200 hours on Sunday, September 18th, 1949. Stark said that he had taken a drink of tetrachloride and lime juice, mistaking it for gin, and treated it as a joke. Earlier that evening, before going down to dinner, the Staff Captain told Stark to take the two Watch Officers (after they had come off watch) to his cabin and help themselves to some gin. From there, it appears that Stark asked Stokes, the Captain's Steward, to find the bottle of gin in the absence of the Staff Captain's Steward.

Stokes went into the Staff Captain's cabin, and from a locked compartment, produced a gin bottle. The young Steward had no way of knowing that the bottle contained fluid used for cleaning cloth material, since there was no marking to show otherwise. He handed the capped "gin" bottle to Stark, and left the quarters. Stark proceeded to pour three gin and limes into the awaiting juice glasses. Unable to wait for the other officers to join him, Stark took a mouthful from one of the glasses.

Ward Room where William Stark would most likely have consumed the lethal dose of carbon tetrachloride

When the other officers arrived, Stark treated the matter humorously and expected no ill consequences. However, he did telephone Dr. O'Mera, the ship's doctor. Stark informed the Staff Captain that he had not smelled the fluid because he had a cold at the time. No one thought that Stark would take a turn for the worse. It wasn't until the next day that he felt ill, and called in the Doctor, who recommended that he rest. On Tuesday, the Doctor advised his transfer to the Hospital. Stark's condition worsened with every hour, until he lapsed into a coma and died from the effects of the poison.

According to Officer Sheehan and Junior Second Officer Wicksteed, Stark seemed very jovial after coming out of the Staff Captain's cabin, where they ran into him. He told them, as he was laughing, that he had accidently drunk carbon tetracloride. Neither of the men realized the seriousness of the situation.

According to Stark, he couldn't understand why the gin and lime did not mix, the lime juice settling on the top, but he dismissed it since he could not smell. He noticed something was wrong when he swallowed the drink, remarking that it tasted pungent, and knowing that it was not gin. No one took it seriously because Stark down-played the whole thing. By the time he was taken to the hospital, it was too late. He died less than four days after accidently swallowing the poison on Thursday, September 22, 1949.

A number of unanswered questions remain: Why didn't Stark seek immediate treatment? Why did he joke to his fellow officers, knowing that he had just swallowed poison? Why didn't anyone insist that he report immediately to the Doctor? Why didn't the Doctor hospitalize Stark immediately? The poisoned officer, his life cut short by this tragedy, apparently remains in familiar surroundings, re-enacting his walks along the deck as part of his job; possibly looking for answers to why his life was cut short so cruelly; or maybe wishing to find someone to share a shot of good gin.

ENGINEER IN A BOILER SUIT

The spectre of a man in a white boiler suit has been seen and heard on numerous occasions below deck. He has been described as being in his forties and dressed in the type of uniform worn by engineers and mechanics in the early years of the ship. Does the mystery man remain on board to repeat his duties which ensured the smooth functioning of the **Queen Mary?**

Maintenance men at work below deck

MAN IN THE OVERALLS

A man in blue-gray overalls, represents yet another spectre that has been spotted below deck. The unearthly vision belongs to a man with jet-black hair, and a long beard, who is dressed in blue-gray overalls.

His appearance is similar to the man in the white boiler suit; possibly another member of the maintenance crew who toiled away below deck. Many times, these workers braved trying conditions to maintain the proper functioning of the **Queen Mary.** He may be continuing his maintenance duties aboard ship, and repeating many of the same patterns and habits he performed while he was alive.

MINI-SKIRTED WOMAN

The poolside spirit of a young, attractive woman in a miniskirt, is sometimes viewed walking down the stairs leading to the pool, and then vanishing behind a pillar. The woman in the miniskirt is not documented in the ship's archives as someone who died in the pool area. However, she may represent someone who died aboard ship who enjoyed spending time in the pool area, where she returns to re-enact a fond memory; or, possibly a guest who died elsewhere, yet decided to come back to a place of peace and contentment while alive.

The haunted pool area where several apparitions have been reported

COOKING UP A TALE OR TWO

Another presence is felt or observed in the kitchen area of the ship. There are several stories which may explain the reason for the occurrences, although two of the stories represent variations of the same theme.

The basic pattern centers on the death of the cook as the result of a fight which broke out during the war years. One story suggests that a certain cook was more interested in feeding the passengers than the crew. As time passed, the crew grew to resent his attitude toward them. After months of the cook's culinary slights and lack of consideration for their needs, several of the crew reportedly tossed him into the oven.

Another account involves a potential mutiny among the American troops being transported aboard ship, resulting in a fight in the kitchen, whereby the cook, who was the object of the crew's ire, was pushed into the heated oven. He died from the resulting burns. The spirit of the cook appears to continue to haunt the kitchen area, possibly still upset that the crew turned on him so viciously. His antics can be heard, seen and felt according to many witnesses. (There is no evidence in the archives to document that such a tragedy actually took place.)

Another possible explanation for the kitchen hauntings, is verified in the ship's archives, and involves a cook named Leonard "Lobster" Horsborough. After serving the **Queen Mary** for 15 years, he died on November 13, 1967 (the **Queen Mary's** last voyage), of complications from a heat stroke and eventual heart failure. He was subsequently buried at sea by Captain Treasure Jones. Although no formal notice was given to passengers of his funeral service, a crowd gathered on the open part of "A" Deck. As word spread, morbid curiosity brought more people to view this solemn event. His remains were given up to the sea, but the circumstances surrounding Horsborough's burial may not have pleased him, considering the lack of respect during his final departure.

Since the event, tales continue to be told of the haunted kitchen area. Perhaps it is the spirit of the cook who was said to have burned alive. Then again, it may be "Lobster," who remains on board the ship he loved. If the **Queen Mary** was his world, and that world was coming to a close, perhaps he decided to exit in flesh, but remain in spirit, cooking and filling orders for other phantom guests.

Main Kitchen area where ghostly sightings have been reported

CARLO GIOVETTI - P.O.W.

Lieutenant Carlo Giovetti, an Italian fighter pilot, and prisoner of war, may have died on board the **Queen Mary.** His spirit was contacted during a seance described later in this book, coming through in a mixture of English and Italian. According to the seance, Carlo had been flying a **Fiat CR42** biplane fighter over North Africa when he was shot down by British pilots. The resulting crash caused extensive injuries to his legs.

As a prisoner of war, he was put aboard the ship, bound for Australia. He witnessed many men die while he was a captive, but could not remember the exact details of his own death. During the seance he described himself as being encased in a canvas bag and being very cold (probably the result of being buried at sea).

The results of the seance, as well as documentation obtained from England, and the ship's archives may provide substantiation to the seance. The ship's archives provide a brief reference to an Italian P.O.W., Faustino

Filippini, who died on the ship on April 17, 1943, and was buried at sea. Could this be "Carlo Giovetti?"

Research also turned up information in the form of a letter from an Italian P.O.W. who survived the war and returned to the ship in the late 1980s. The survivor states that he boarded the *Queen Mary* in May of 1941 at Suez and was taken to Sydney, Australia. He believed his group to be the first Italian P.O.W.'s to be carried in the *Queen Mary.* The P.O.W.'s were loaded aboard in cargo nets and hoisted on deck. They had hammocks to sleep in, and were only allowed on deck after the ship left port. No duties were assigned while on board, due to the poor physical condition of the P.O.W.'s. Their clothing and shoes were ragged and torn, and they were not issued new clothing until after they arrived at the P.O.W. camp in Australia. It was a stifling voyage. This information corroborates Giovetti's seance story regarding the conditions afforded P.O.W.'s aboard the *Queen Mary.*

The Queen Mary as a troop transport

Additional data suggest that many Italian and German P.O.W.'s died during transport, their bodies buried at sea. Giovetti, if that is his real name, probably died on his way to a P.O.W. camp, his spirit apparently tied to the *Queen Mary.* Perhaps the memory is so unpleasant that he cannot

24

break loose from it; or, he simply wants his story told before he can move on.

MISS TURNER

The friendly spirit of a Miss Turner also came through in a seance. According to the account, she was a freckled, auburn-haired woman, in charge of the 700-line switchboard located on "B" Deck. It was the largest switchboard installed on an ocean liner. It became immediately apparent on the maiden voyage that she was in way over her head.

Main swithcboard in operation—the spirit of a former operator was contacted during a seance

According to historical records aboard the **Queen Mary**, there were so many calls to and from the ship during her London-New York crossing, that a number of them were never able to be placed. An inspection of the Ship's records, do not list the names of all personnel on the maiden voyage. Therefore, verification that a woman named Turner worked the switchboard is still lacking. Why she remains on the ship is anybody's guess—perhaps to complete the backlog of unfinished calls, or continue as operator for the spirit world.

MRS. KILBURN

The spirit of a Mrs. Kilburn also came through in a seance. She was described as being trim in her gray uniform with starched white cuffs, and very efficient. She was in charge of the stewardesses and bellboys during the voyages. Going to sea was nothing new to her, since her family had served the Cunard Line for three generations.

Kilburn was a nurse and schoolmistress before joining the staff aboard the **Queen Mary.** A strong-willed woman, and stickler for detail, she demanded efficiency and neatness from her staff. Her philosophy was very simple: Smile if you want; otherwise be efficient. As with Miss Turner, there has been no verification, as yet, of either her name on the crew manifest, or her death aboard ship. Perhaps Mrs. Kilburn remains to make sure everyone puts his/her best foot forward!

THE LADY IN WHITE

Although there is no historical documentation available about the Lady in White , she is frequently seen in spirit aboard ship. She appears to have haunted the Main Lounge (now the Queen's Salon), and was seen

Main Lounge: The favorite haunt for the Lady in White

from time to time waltzing into the Lounge wearing a backless, white evening gown. As the stories went, she either strolled over to the grand piano as if listening to a ghostly rendition on the keys, or danced by herself for a few moments before vanishing into thin air in front of startled witnesses.

An interesting twist to the story involves the grand piano. Several years back, the piano was moved from the Main Lounge, to Sir Winston's Piano Bar. Although the Lady in White ceased showing herself in the Lounge, she has begun appearing at Sir Winston's. Apparently, as the piano moved, so did the Lady.

The spirit of the Lady in White represents one of many such phenomena seen aboard the ship. These manifestations may be residual energy resulting from an actual death where a spirit returns to a specific location due to fond memories, to repeat certain behaviors; or, as in the case of the Lady in White, become attached to a specific object—the grand piano.

OTHER ACTIVITY ON BOARD

A number of other incidents of paranormal activity have been reported over the years by security guards, staff, crew and paranormal investigators. In fact, security on board have often been troubled by the doors aboard the ship which appear to have a mind of their own.

For unknown reasons, doors that are locked one minute, mysteriously become unlocked the next, triggering alarm lights in the security office. This occurs most frequently with the doors near the swimming pool. Inspections have been unable to turn up any culprits, but someone or some THING appears to be playing tricks on them.

Numerous other accounts of strange phenomena, include: inexplicable noises, such as the sound of footsteps when no one is there; banging and hammering, as if someone is working on long-since removed equipment; voices; enigmatic cold spots and winds in air-tight areas; lights going on and off of their own accord; and objects disappearing, or being moved—the list continues to grow!

WHO'S COUNTING

Historical sources place the death toll aboard the *Queen Mary* at

55, since it was launched in 1936. Of the 55 documented cases, 39 were passengers and 16 were crew. The ages range from a child who died at birth, to a 77-year-old woman, The deaths have resulted from: Heart attacks; people jumping overboard; falls; an overdose; accidental poisoning; being crushed to death; and natural causes.

An area where two guests reportedly fell to their deaths

Psychic investigators believe that the death toll may actually be in the hundreds, if the deaths of P.O.W.'s are considered. During the war years, because the ship was used as a troop transport as well as carrying prisoners of war, unconfirmed stories tell of suffocating heat below deck, resulting in frequent deaths and burials at sea. Finally, though accidental, the **Queen Mary** was involved in the sinking of the **HMS Curacoa** on October 2, 1942, resulting in the deaths of 338 seaman. According to the records, while the **Queen Mary** approached the Scottish coastline with 10,000 American troops aboard, she came in contact with a small destroyer escort which intended to protect the **Queen Mary** from submarine attack, if it became necessary. Leading the entourage was the 450-foot-long, 4,290-ton British anti-aircraft cruiser, the **Curacoa.** Tactical procedures called for the destroyers to form a protective cordon around the **Queen Mary.**

Suddenly, before anyone realized the danger, the **Queen Mary,** still on her usual zig-zag course as a matter of standard wartime operating procedure, hit the unsuspecting **Curacoa** at high speed. The force of the

Queen Mary impacting the *Curacoa,* 150 feet forward of the cruiser's stern, spun the ship broadside to the *Queen Mary's* bow, which sliced the *Curacoa* in half, like a stick of butter. Many of the *Curacoa's* crew died instantly below deck, drowning in the cold seas as the ship sank.

Two crewmen were able to make their way to safety from below deck by crawling into a hatch leading into one of the vessel's funnels. They reached the side of the sinking ship, and slid down her hull into the icy water.

The crew and soldiers on the upper decks of the *Queen Mary* could only watch in horror as the *Curacoa* went under. Some of those who watched, had the sensibility to begin throwing life preservers to the stranded men below. The *Curacoa* sank in less than five minutes. The *Queen Mary* radioed for help, but could not risk the lives of 10,000 men by attempting to rescue the remaining survivors, and was forced to continue on. Sixty-two of the 400 men aboard the *Curacoa* miraculously survived the collision.

The *Queen Mary,* though suffering damage to her bow, managed to make it to port without further incident. Perhaps a few of the victims of the Curacoa remain attached to the *Queen Mary,* seeking retribution— since a wartime investigation laid one-third of the blame for the accident on the *Queen Mary* personnel.

The Pre-War Main Ballroom was fitted as a troop hospital

There are those, including historians and psychics, who feel that the men who worked or were forced to occupy the space well below deck, sometimes suffered great hardship due to the intense heat and emotional flare-ups. In addition there are indications that the prisoners of war may have been occasionally mistreated while being transported during war time. Apparently, while at sea, a few of those who died were kept in a make-shift morgue aboard ship, their bodies refrigerated until the ship reached port. Others were buried at sea.

GUEST GHOST SIGHTINGS

Over the years, many guests have responded to the haunting questions of mysterious happenings aboard the *Queen Mary* by filling out questionnaires or sending in letters which documented their experiences. These responses in the ship's archives have produced some very interesting information, which follows:

T.L.G. AND R.B. OF CALIFORNIA - At eleven p.m., we went to our room, B123, located next to the Coke machine. As we entered, we saw a man standing by our bed. He was about 5'11" tall, broad- shouldered, and wearing a black, navy coat (porter/pea coat) and a black cap. He remained for a few seconds and then disappeared, We were not frightened as much as caught off guard. We remained in the room, and he came back to visit one more time. We have no idea was he was doing there, or what he may have been looking for.

The Haunted First Class Nursery

L.S. OF CALIFORNIA - My friend and I, while on the guided tour, which included the nursery area, heard a noise at the door to the nursery, that the guide couldn't open. It rattled by itself and made clicking noises. Also, several times during the tour, I felt as if someone was constantly tugging at my purse and shirt, even though no one was standing next to me. Another time, I had the strongest feeling that I was being followed in one of the hallways. Later on during the tour, as I was standing at the end of the line, and the air was completely still, I felt something touch my hair. It gave me the chills since I looked around and there was no one to be seen.

H.H. OF DELAWARE - While taking the tour, I stopped at the pool and decided to toss a penny in for good luck. As I was throwing the penny I heard what seemed like someone whispering to me, telling me that it was not nice to throw things in the pool. It was a distinct sound that seemed to pop inside my head. I looked around, and no one else could have said it.

S.N. OF CALIFORNIA - While I was staying in Room A138, I heard a knock at the door. When I opened it, there was no one there. I looked down the hall, and it was deserted. I thought I was hearing things. However, later that night it happened again. There was a faint knock at the door which I went to check on. Again, there was no one at the door or in the hallway. It was a very strange feeling.

L.B. OF OREGON - My family and I were on the bridge looking around. I wandered off by myself to the chart room.

The Haunted Bridge

As I was finding the **Queen Mary** on a map they have in the room, I had the sensation that someone was tugging at the back of my shirt. Thinking it was a family member, I turned quickly, and felt a chill. There was no one around. I left the room at once, with goosebumps all over my body. This was the first time anything like that ever happened to me.

M.H. OF OHIO- Last night I was awakened from my sleep by the sensation that the ship was pitching or rolling. I do not drink, so I couldn't attribute it to that. I am familiar with traveling at sea, and being that the ship is protected from the open sea, and that the water was stable all week, it couldn't have been caused by currents. I reasoned that maybe I was taken back in time to when the ship was at sea. I couldn't explain it any other way.

H.H. OF CALIFORNIA- While exploring the sun deck by the elevators, I heard the distinct sound of footsteps running up the stairs. Then, out of the corner of my eye I noticed that the porthole at the top of the stairs had suddenly gone dark and it looked as if rain was beating against the glass. As I heard the footsteps coming closer, I turned away from the porthole toward the sound, but no one was there. When I looked back at the porthole, it was normal once again. The experience gave me butterflies in my stomach. After that, I had a strong desire to go to the Engine Room, even though I had never been on the ship before. It was as if I was being led there by some force.

G.F. OF OREGON - After visiting water-tight door number 26, I saw the back of a man in dark blue work clothes walking through a narrow hallway. He didn't look like he belonged on the ship, so I attempted to follow him. I looked everywhere, but I never found him, or anyone who looked like him.

J.M. OF CALIFORNIA- I was at the Purser's Desk when I caught a brief glimpse out of the corner of my eye, of someone or something moving. It was there for a second, and then it was gone. I looked around, but could not find anything. I was positive that it was not my reflection, but I don't know exactly *what* it was.

C.L. OF CALIFORNIA - At the Sundeck exhibit, beyond the stairwell heading down, I got a mental image of a male between 20-25 years-old, wearing a blue mechanic's uniform. After a few seconds, the feeling left me and the area felt cold and empty.

D.D. OF CALIFORNIA- In the pool area, I saw a huge puff of steam rise from nowhere. As quickly as it appeared, it diminished. Right after that, I saw a small girl across the pool. I asked about her, but apparently I was the only one who saw her. She had dark hair, and was wearing a white and blue dress with a square collar and puffed sleeves. She looked like a hologram image that just disappeared in front of me. I'm not sure anyone else saw it.

P.M. OF TEXAS - I awoke from a deep sleep to the sound of snoring coming from the other side of the bed where my husband was sleeping. At first I thought it was him, so I listened. He was quiet and asleep. I heard the snoring again, and this time I woke my husband up. He dismissed the entire incident and went back to sleep. But, I did hear *something* on the other side of me, and it wasn't my husband.

J.M. OF CALIFORNIA- While touring the Sun Deck exhibit area, I noticed a middle-aged lady near the piano. She wore a brown dress with a white lace collar, and a light green sweater, with a gold pin. I turned my head for a second, looked back, and she had vanished. I don't know how she could have gotten inside the exhibit and then out so quickly. I'm positive it wasn't my imagination.

D.G. OF CALIFORNIA - My friend and I were alone on the top deck. We went downstairs to the deck below, and heard footsteps as if coming from a large group of people on the deck where we had been. Since we didn't recall seeing anyone on that deck prior to going down, we decided to go up and check. As we looked around, we got the chills. The deck was empty!

I.G & M.G OF CALIFORNIA- We stayed in Room A110. When we checked in, I distinctly remember leaving our luggage on a chair, away from where we walk. Later that night, when I went to the bathroom, I tripped over my luggage. Somehow, after going to bed, our luggage had been moved several feet from its original position, blocking access to the bathroom. My wife denied moving it, but *someone* did.

A.C. OF CALIFORNIA- I awoke from a deep sleep around midnight. I saw a figure walking near my daughter's sleeping bag toward the door. Thinking it was my sister, I called out. There was no answer. It was then that I noticed my sister was lying next to me. I sat up in bed and watched the person in white walk through the door! I was unaware at the time of the ship's ghosts.

V.G. OF CALIFORNIA- I stayed in Room M029, and would like to relate two curious events which took place while I was on board. While I was shaving, my kit fell off the shelf in front of the bathroom sink. No one else was in the room at the time, and I examined the shelf closely—it was straight and quite secure. The second incident occurred when I was drawing the bath for my wife. I couldn't budge the faucet. My wife tried to help, but both of us couldn't turn the water on. Trying one last time, the faucet turned on easily.

Strange occurrences have been reported in several bathrooms

A.F. AND C.F. OF VIRGINIA - We stayed in room B462. As my husband was brushing his teeth, he felt a tightening in his chest, as well as the sensation of someone watching him. When he came into the bedroom, he saw a lady between 25-35 years-old standing near our baby. She had brown hair and was wearing a long, white camisole-type gown. When I looked again, she had vanished.

LOCATION OF SIGHTINGS ABOARD THE QUEEN MARY

Access Legend

W   -   Walking tour - self-guided
LA   -   Limited access: part of ship's tour
NA   -   Not accessible

Sightings Legend

1. Sports Deck - Sir Winston's Piano Bar: LADY IN WHITE {W}
2. Sports Deck - MISS TURNER [W]
3. Sports Deck - WILLIAM STARK'S room [W]
4. Sports Deck - The haunted Bridge area [W]
5. Sun Deck - The haunted exhibits area [W]
6. Promenade Deck - Original sighting of the LADY IN WHITE [W]
7. Promenade Deck - Main Ballroom [W]
8. Main Deck - Likely spot where passengers viewed LEONARD HORSBOROUGH'S burial at sea [W]
9. Main Deck - Children's Nursery [NA]
10. "A" Deck - Location of the "Old Spice" encounter [W]
11. "A" Deck - Likely spot where LEONARD HORSBOROUGH was buried at sea [W]
12. "A" Deck - Location of a haunted stairway [W]
13. "B" Deck - Male and female hospital rooms [NA]
14. "R" Deck - Main Kitchen area [NA]
15. "R" Deck - First Class Main Dining Room [LA]
16. "C" Deck - This area served as the ship's morgue [NA]
17. "C" Deck - The ship's hospital area (male and female ward rooms) [NA]
18. "C" Deck - Catwalk overlooking the Boiler Room [W]
19. "C" Deck - The haunted pool area and dressing rooms [LA]
20. "G" Deck - The haunted Engine Room and Shaft Alley [W]
21 "G" Deck - Water-tight door number 13 [W]
22. "G" Deck - Boiler Room encounters [NA]

*** Several hotel rooms on the Main Deck, and "A" and "B" decks are reportedly haunted

SPORTS DECK

SUN DECK

PROMENADE DECK

MAIN DECK

"A" DECK

"B" DECK

"R" DECK

"C" DECK

"G" DECK

C.S. OF CALIFORNIA - While I was walking on a self-guided tour, I approached water-tight door number 13. I heard someone whistling, and went to look for the source. I checked all around, but I couldn't find where it was coming from. There was no one down there except me, Also, near emergency steering in the Engine Room, I heard someone running, but I could not locate a soul. Something strange is happening below deck.

S.S. OF CALIFORNIA- Out of the corner of my eye, I saw a man in a blue shirt, walk toward a long hallway. As I turned to follow him, he vanished into thin air. He looked like he didn't belong there.

H.V. OF CALIFORNIA - I was awakened from my sleep and observed the image of a person standing in front of my bed. There were no apparent physical features, but it appeared to be holding a flashlight, with a light shining out of it that was brighter than the form itself. I watched as the image swayed back and forth. When I called my roommate, the vision backed up. I called again and the vision backed up even further, toward the door. I reached for the light switch and tried to turn it on. The light switch seemed to spark and wouldn't turn on all the way. Finally, my roommate woke up; the light came on, and whatever it was, was gone. We slept with the TV on the rest of the night. It was a great experience, and I had a lot of fun!

A typical first class room

S.M. OF OREGON - I was in the pool area and saw a tall woman dressed in an old wedding gown. Her hair was in a bun and she was with a nicely-dressed boy in a suit. It sent chills down my spine, because as quickly as they appeared, they vanished into thin air! I know I was not hallucinating.

P.T. OF CALIFORNIA - I was alone in Shaft Alley near water-tight door number 13. I decided to talk to John Pedder, because I heard his story and felt sorry for him and the way he died. I told him how lonely it must have been to die by himself. As I stood in the middle of the door, and moved back and forth a few times, I saw something move out of the corner of my eye. It was a brief glimpse of someone or something, maybe John. I did not feel threatened, nor did it make me fearful. To be honest, it was not the first time something like this has happened down there. I have had a similar experience before.

E.B. & B.B. OF CALIFORNIA - We spent the night in Room B401. While we were relaxing, we both heard taps or a light knocking on our suite door. I asked who it was, but there was no reply. I got up to open the door, and when I looked out, there was no one to be seen. This happened later on that night with the same results. Maybe it was someone playing a practical joke, although I think we knew it was something else.

M.F. OF CALIFORNIA - While on the ship, my husband and I occasionally joked about someone following us, or of hearing a thumping sound coming from below. Actually, if we would have been confronted by anything out of the ordinary, we probably would have been frightened. When we went through water-tight door number 13 in Shaft Alley, knowing the story of John Pedder, we jokingly asked him if he would like to join us on our little self-guided tour. When we were leaving the ship I noticed that my husband had a spot of black grease on his face, as if someone put the tip of their finger up against his face and pressed. We could never figure out how the grease got there. Maybe John left his calling card!

     ** If, after *your* visit aboard the ***Queen Mary,*** you have a story to tell about a strange or unexplainable experience, please fill out the attached form at the back of this book.

WALKING TOUR INTO THE UNKNOWN

     Several ghost-hunting tours have been conducted on the ***Queen Mary*** since the late 1980s by Richard Senate, a professional paranormal investigator, and his wife, Debbie Christenson Senate, a psychic. Excerpts from some of the participants who attended one of these tours, provide insights into the phenomena observed and/or noted aboard the ship. They also represent the impressions of average people who spent a rather harrowing night aboard the ship in search of its ghosts.

Because this was a special ghost tour, the participants were allowed in areas of the ship which are not normally accessible to the public. The diagrams of the ship presented within this book, illustrate areas where sightings have occurred. They provide information as to which areas can be reached by way of a self-guided tour, or the ship's guided tour. Note that some areas are inaccessible to the public.

TOUR GUEST # 1

As we walked through the Captain's cabin, I had the strangest sensation of getting seasick, as if the ship were moving. It got so bad, I had to leave and go outside for fresh air. Once I went outside, I felt better.

Another situation occurred while I was walking through the Main Ballroom area. When I walked inside, I came face-to-face with a cold spot or cold front in one area of the floor. All around me the air was warm, so it was hard to explain why this one place was so cold. I checked for drafts or air vents and found nothing that would explain the sensation.

There was also a room where I felt very lonely at the end of the crew quarters, portside of the big hole. In addition, the catwalk above the boiler room scared me, and I am not afraid of heights. Finally, I got chills when I entered the Boiler Room, and at the center, below the catwalk.

TOUR GUEST # 2

There were several areas we visited as part of the tour, where I felt uneasy. One place was the pool area, which kind of spooked me. In particular, I had a very heavy and weighty feeling when I passed through the pool dressing rooms, and in general, when walking around the pool area. Another area which felt "unearthly" was in the First Class bathroom. I wanted to leave the minute I walked inside.

TOUR GUEST # 3

While on the tour we went to the pool area which was very eerie, especially by the women's bathroom. I felt a chill like I'd never felt before. The changing room, especially, feels very active.

The eerie Dressing Room in the pool area - Some psychics consider this to be the gateway to another dimension

While I was wandering through the ship's artifact display area, which at one time was either part of the engine room, or where a smoke stack once was, something poked my friend. Maybe there is [a ghost] there because all the old items from the ship are on display.

Finally, when we got back to our room on board the ship at 4:00 a.m. I sat on my bed with the dowsing rods, and felt a spirit in my room—a woman between 15-25, whose name began with the letter "J." She was friendly and I felt her presence with us in the morning.

TOUR GUEST # 4

While walking through the pool area, I saw a girl standing there, as clear as day. She appeared to be from the 1940s, and seemed to be cheerful and content. My feeling is that this person once sailed on the **Queen Mary** as a young lady, maybe in her early twenties, and after dying, many years later, comes back to a time when she was happiest, and very carefree.

Sketch by eyewitness

She is mischievous, and sometimes likes to play hide-and-seek with people rather than trying to frighten them. I sense that she is there all the time, watching and waiting, giggling behind a pillar. She's excited that so many people come to visit the pool area to see her.

TOUR GUEST # 5

When the tour group visited Shaft Alley at 3:30 a.m., dowsing was very active by two different doorways. One was where John Pedder died. We thought we heard footsteps by the door. The guard who was with us said he had never *seen* a ghost, but the he has *felt* John's presence.

TOUR GUEST # 6

While walking around the pool area, each time I looked from the guide to the pool, I noticed a red light in the same place. On the catwalk over the boiler room, I waited until most of the people were off the bridge before I crossed. I felt something nudge me; it felt like a ripple going up my spine. The whole boiler room was very creepy, and I felt like I was not wanted there. I felt very unsettling things on the Promenade, as if something was just not right. I was tired and drained being in that area of the ship.

TOUR GUEST # 7

When I walked through the doors to the pool area, I got chilled. My whole body shook—there is definitely something there! I also got a sad feeling when we went to the boiler room, and heard strange noises. There are many areas where you feel uneasy, as if you are constantly being watched.

TOUR GUEST # 8

I did not feel comfortable in the Boiler Room. When I visited the pool area, I was overwhelmed by a sense of hardship, fear and strife, as if people had lived there in crowded conditions and several had died. As I walked around the pool, the name Julie Aura came into my head. I sensed that she drowned, and her body was found unclothed. I felt that she was 24-25 years old, and had either traveled in Second Class with her aunt, or had an affair with and older, married man in First Class, where they met late at night by the pool. [There is no substantiation in the ship's archives of any person drowning].

TOUR GUEST # 9

I felt a tightness in my chest when I passed through the dressing room area by the pool. A sadness came over me there—someone crying perhaps? I felt the same sadness and pressure on my chest in shaft alley.

TOUR GUEST # 10

It was exciting to participate in the seance. I enjoyed the entity of Clara that came through Debbie. I felt so much pity for her—she was so naive. Toward the end of the seance, I felt a sharp pain, a pinching on my neck, which hurt me. I called out to the others. The name Sarah Longwoods came to my mind, and I called her name. It was a wonderful experience.

TOUR GUEST # 11

Upon entering the pool area, I was immediately drawn to the steps on the left, where I felt a strong sense of dread and anxiety. When I went down the stairs, I stood at the corner of the pool. While standing there, I experienced the same feelings I had upon entering the pool area. I also felt a cold spot over to the side. There was a strong feeling coming from the room under the stairs. In the dressing room I had a strong negative feeling at the very end in the shower and toilet room.

Entering the boiler room, I felt something at the first railing, and saw a strange haze between a beam and the wall. After that, I walked around the room, then came back to the same railing, but the feeling wasn't quite as strong.

Strange sounds continue to be heard in the Boiler Room

In the Officer's Quarters, I felt something in the chained-off hallway. I walked over to the area, and felt a cold spot in and above the chair closest to the exit. It seemed as if there was someone sitting and watching me.

TOUR GUEST # 12

During the seance, I sensed that there are many people, who for some reason have not realized that they have "crossed over." The Boiler Room gave me an eerie feeling when we went down there.

When we went to the pool area, I thought I saw an older woman swimming in a black, one-piece bathing suit, and wearing a white bathing cap—the name Adelle came to me.

Last night, about 1:00 a.m., after I returned to my room, I heard a moan in the bathroom that sounded like Carlo from the seance. Also, as I went to sleep, my bed appeared to be rocking gently.

TOUR GUEST # 13

The tour eventually went to the pool area. It was there that I saw a woman standing by the side of the pool. She had brown hair, and was wearing a white dress. She appeared to be petite and young. I took my eyes off of her to see if other people were watching. By the time I turned around to look again, which was only a matter of a few seconds, she disappeared.

The pool area and eyewitness sketches

TOUR GUEST # 14

After the seance and the tour, I had a few impressions of the time I spent with the group. The Boiler Room seemed to be a deep, dark dungeon and a scary place to be. I learned during the seance that there were more ghosts here than John Pedder and the woman in the pool. My general feeling is that there are many souls trapped aboard the ship.

TOUR GUEST # 15

I received consistent readings from my dowsing rods of spirits in three places that we visited on the ship. The first area was in the side hallway between cabins B421 and B423; the second was in the staircase between the main deck and "A" Deck, top half, aft, starboard corner; and the third, was in the First Class pool area in the forward, starboard corner of the pool. While in the pool area with the group, I got a sudden chill on the back of my neck.

TOUR GUEST # 16

During the ghost tour, I got very negative feelings in a couple of areas. One area was located near the left-hand corner of the pool area, and the other area was in the ballroom, where I had a very strong feeling of someone watching me. There was another area in the Officer's Quarters, where it felt as if a force of some kind was blocking me near the chairs.

TOUR GUEST # 17

While we were walking in the pool area, my friend went out in the corridor and said that she felt a presence next to her. As it turned out, this corridor led to the Boiler Room. As I walked down the corridor to the boiler room, I felt a strange chill. While in the room, the silence and emptiness caused my mind to wander, allowing me to imagine what it must have looked like when the ship was in operation. I also felt something in Shaft 7, Door 13, which was the area where crew member Jonathan Pedder was crushed during a routine drill. According to tour guides, there have been numerous sightings of a man in white overalls below deck, especially in the boiler room area.

TOUR GUEST #18

In the pool area, down below the diving board, on the right-hand side, I saw an image of a woman. As walked through the First Class Dining Room, I smelled flowers... Gardenias? In the boiler room, I heard sounds of metal hitting metal, as if men were working. I heard a man yelling, "Turn that off, damnit, turn it off!" In the Third Class Dining Room, my friend felt a presence by the piano—he sensed it was a man who resented the intrusion. My hair stood on end.

Debbie Senate felt that the presence was a male, and there was a barrier she could not break through. The image I got was of a male in his mid-40s-50s, brown hair, dark vest, open shirt, with light brown clothing.

My friend felt someone watching us in the Second Class Dining Room. Richard felt a tingling sensation in the pool area, and the tour guide reported seeing the ghost of a girl in a green mini-skirt in this same area. One member of the team saw a red light in the pool.

DEBBIE CHRISTENSON SENATE

Debbie toured the swimming pool area, and was stunned to see a red glow in one of the dressing rooms, and a figure swimming under the water. The image didn't last long. Others in the group saw bubbles appear in the water.

Phantom sounds of children playing and guests strolling
have been reported on many of the decks

Debbie and I walked the darkened decks of the moored ocean liner. It was almost 4:00 a.m., and there was no one around. Suddenly, we heard footsteps on the deck above us. Debbie turned to me and said, "Those footsteps are made by ghosts." They seemed so real, I doubted this; and since we were close to a stairway, I leaped up the steps to confront our fellow night owls; however, there was no one to be seen—we were alone!

OTHERWORLDLY HAPPENINGS

There are literally hundreds of other stories about ghosts and paranormal activity aboard the *Queen Mary.* A few of the more unique encounters have been directly recounted or paraphrased.

Certain corridors are reportedly haunted

A CONCESSIONAIRE MEETS AN UNKNOWN FORCE

On "A" Deck near the stern of the ship, next to a stairway, the concessionaire and his friend were walking down the corridor late one night, when they noticed a tray near one of the cabin doors. As they approached the stairway, the tray literally flew down the corridor before coming to rest 40 or 50 feet away from them. Frozen in their tracks, they felt a rush of cold air pass through them. Within seconds, a sign hanging on the corridor wall was ripped off, and flung onto the carpeting. They saw no one, and didn't wait around long enough to encounter any further activity.

THE TOUR GUIDE AND THE GHOSTLY CHILDREN

A tour guide related his story of hearing the laughter of children and the sound of footsteps on the deck above him as he was walking up the aft stairwell. The sound continued until he neared the top of the flight of stairs. The sound of laughter was such that he knew he would come across the children any moment. As he reached the top of the stairs he heard the laughter, as if they were next to him—but he was alone. After a few moments, the sound stopped as quickly as it had begun. This incident made for a rather hair-raising experience.

The ghostly sounds of children have been reported in several areas

A DOG IS MAN'S BEST FRIEND... UNTIL IT MEETS A GHOST

Another story involves a security guard with a dog patrolling "G" Deck. As they made their way along the deck, the dog stopped, snarled and began growling. As the guard urged the dog on, it began to whine, and wouldn't budge from its position. Finally, the sound of something metal rolling toward them prompted the Guard and his dog to immediately flee the area. As chance would have it, the incident took place in Shaft Alley where John Pedder was killed.

HOW MUCH IS A STORY WORTH?

A journalist decided to roam the dark corridors of the ship late one night, in search of ghosts—something he did not believe in. In the early morning hours, while being shut off in Shaft Alley by design, he heard a loud clanging sound, as if someone were banging on the pipes. When he approached the area from where the sound emanated, it stopped—when he backed away, the sound began again. As he moved away from the sound, his retreat was blocked by an oil drum which had mysteriously appeared out of nowhere. He began to panic.

The Engine Room has been the scene of frequent sightings

Trying to beat a hasty retreat, he proceeded up the passageway. Feeling his way back in the darkness, two more oil drums blocked his path. Overcoming those obstacles, he walked cautiously along a catwalk, only to encounter an ominous presence. Someone or something was coming toward him, but he couldn't see anything. After quickly shifting directions, he felt a sudden rush of wind in an airtight area brush by him. Stopping "dead" in his tracks, he heard the faint sound of men talking. No one else should have been down there. Within a short period of time, all the voices trailed off, except one. That is when he heard some unintelligible words followed by a more distinct phrase, "Turn the lights off!"

After his ordeal ended, he asked the security guard about the voices he heard. Could there have been other people below with him? The response was an emphatic "No." Apparently the closest person to him during that time was two decks away. The guard confirmed that others claimed to have heard ghostly voices in the Shaft Alley area as well. We don't know if the journalist changed his mind about ghosts, but it seems that someone was certainly trying to persuade him!

HAUNTED HOUSEKEEPING

A woman working in the housekeeping office on "A" Deck, related the story of an uncanny event which took place while she was on duty. She described seeing "someone" wearing a white dress, standing by Frame 135 elevator in the "A" Deck service area. The housekeeper was having a hectic day, and thought it was just another employee performing her routine duties, even though the woman looked odd, and transparent.

She remembers glancing away for a heartbeat before deciding to take a more thorough look. In that brief moment, the ghostly woman vanished. There were no sounds of footsteps, or of the elevator being used. The housekeeper was alone, left only with the image of the apparition.

A TALE OF TWO WOMEN

Two female guests became caught up in ghostly room encounter. While occupying Room M202, both women were awakened by the sounds of people putting clothes away in an adjoining closet. The banging and thumping were so loud, that they were about to get up to complain. Suddenly the commotion stopped, and the two women went back to sleep.

In the morning, they decided to walk by the cabin where the sounds had come from the night before, hoping to discover who the noisemakers were. What they found, shocked them—there was no cabin or closet. The adjoining area next to where they slept was open space next to the bulkhead!

The next night, again, both women were awakened. This time, by the sound of someone constantly going to the bathroom. They heard footsteps repeatedly cross their cabin floor, enter the bathroom and shut the door. They looked around but couldn't find a "living soul." One of the women refused to take a bath, saying that the faucet emitted weird sounds, and the room had an unnerving, eerie quality to it.

AN ORDER FROM ANOTHER DIMENSION

Bizarre things occur quite often on the **Queen Mary.** However, for one female employee, they happened with greater frequency. According to her, most of the strange events took place on the lower decks: Dishes flew around, she heard knocking on a table when no one was there, and tables shook while she read the newspaper.

On one occasion, in the Promenade Cafe, the employee noticed a woman dressed in 1940s clothes sitting at a coffee table. The clothes were a "dead give-away," since the 40s "retro" look was not fashionable at the time. The employee took her eyes off the oddly dressed woman for a moment, then turned back to find that she had vanished. After looking around without success, she knew "they" were playing tricks on her again!

Deserted Promenade Deck

CREW MEMBERS BELIEVE

A few years after the ship arrived from her last voyage, people began to talk secretly about strange, spooky things happening around the ship. People reported seeing shadows, hearing voices and noises when no one else was around—things no one could explain after each search for evidence proved futile.

People began reporting that they saw things around the pool area: Wet footprints, as if someone just got out of the water; a woman in white who walked barefoot by the pool and disappeared; and an angry cook who walked around slamming doors and making noises. These kinds of stories date back to the 1930s when the ship was first commissioned, and there were at least half a dozen separate sightings.

BEYOND A SHADOW OF DOUBT?

One employee who worked on the ship for a number of years, saw plenty of things that couldn't be explained, such as plates flying across the room in the cafeteria. He was positive there was a ghost in the main kitchen area. He was also matter-of-fact in stating that there are places the crew won't go because they are frightened—like the wardrobe area, where the ship's morgue was supposed to be. People say that it's eerie and cold in there. The exhibit hall seems to be another place where people hear things when no one else is around—voices and other noises.

The employee continues, talking about the lady by the pool who is there one second, then disappears. That's just one of the places the employees won't go alone. Another is the Engine Room which also seems to have its own, not so pleasant feeling. This employee is positive that there are spirits on the ship. To him, it's a matter of "live and let live." In fact, he says, "Some of the places have different feelings from others; scarier, where you get goosebumps or feel cold."

LIVING IN HARMONY WITH THE DEAD

Another employee actually *likes* the idea of spending time with the spirits. He mentioned working in the main kitchen and definitely feeling a presence keeping an eye on him. He also feels cold spots where there are no drafts or ventilation, and is firmly convinced that there are people "not of this world," watching him.

He doesn't care what people think, and he isn't afraid, saying, "People shouldn't be frightened of what they can't see. The ship has its own feeling, as if you are in another world, but you get used to it. Leave them be and they will let you do your thing."

THE TOUR GUIDE AND THE POOL GUEST GHOST

One day, while a tour guide was alone by the swimming pool waiting for a group to arrive, she spotted an elderly woman standing by the edge of the pool. The woman appeared to be in her sixties and was wearing

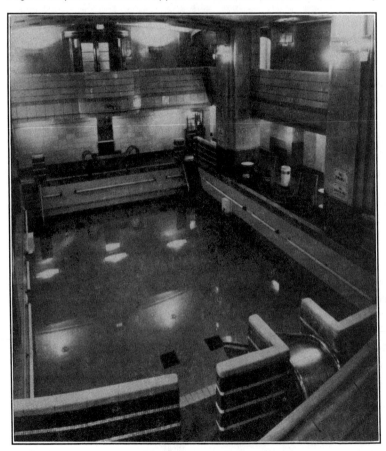

Another view of the haunted pool

an old-fashioned, one-piece bathing suit and bathing cap; her curly hair protruding from under the cap. There were two disconcerting problems:

The elderly woman appeared to the guide in *black and white*; and secondly, was about to dive into a pool that had no water (it had been drained). Thinking the strange-looking woman might be a tourist who accidently wandered into the pool area, the guide's immediate reaction was to call security.

Before summoning help however, the guide decided to turn and warn the woman not to jump in. In that brief moment, the elderly woman disappeared. The confused guide immediately began checking the doors— They were all locked. A thorough inspection revealed no trace of the strange-looking woman. Although skeptical about ghosts, the guide was convinced that what she saw was real. As an afterthought, she reasoned that if it *was* a ghost, perhaps it was someone who enjoyed the pool area during a cruise, and was returning to the place that brought her pleasure.

GOING UP?

Another tour guide, while closing up, was walking into the south alley where there are two sets of escalators. He was coming up one esca-lator, when just a few steps from the top, he had a distinct feeling that someone was behind him. Sure that he was the last person on the shift, he turned slowly to find a man standing on the escalator. The man had black hair, white skin, large, dark eyes and a nicely kept black beard. He was wearing dirty blue overalls as if he had been repairing something. He wasn't threatening, and didn't try to communicate. He just stood there quietly.

The guide turned to watch where he was going as he reached the top of the escalator, and stepped aside to let the man pass. When the guide turned, the man in the dirty blue overalls had disappeared. The guide didn't see the man appear or disappear, but in a matter of seconds, he was there and gone.

THE PLUMBER AND THE POOL PARTY

A "routine" plumbing job turned out to be anything but routine. While working the graveyard shift, a plumber on his way to the shop, which is located close to the pool, distinctly heard voices accompanied by the sounds of water splashing, glasses clinking and a ball bouncing.

His first inclination was to think that guests had made their way to the pool and were having a late-night party. However, as he turned the corner and reached the pool area, there was no one in sight; no movement in the water; and no glasses or ball to be seen. Thinking that his mind was playing tricks on him, or someone else was, he went back to work. A short time later, he heard the same sounds again. Cautiously approaching the pool area, he looked in again and saw no one. He called Security, but nothing or no one was ever found.

THE GHOSTLY ENGINEER

Another story surrounding Shaft Alley involves two couples aboard the ship. According to the story, one couple came up the escalator from Shaft Alley and reported to maintenance personnel that a man in white coveralls had told them that he had dropped his wrench, and asked them to bring him another one.

A short time later, a second couple came up the escalator with the same story for the maintenance personnel—an engineer in white coveralls told them that he had lost a wrench and needed another one. The description of the coveralls didn't match the present-day uniform, and the bizarre nature of the engineer's request from below deck caused them to investigate. There was no man to be found anywhere. He had vanished, presumably without finding a replacement wrench.

THE PSYCHIC AND THE QUEEN

Several prominent psychic investigators have visited the *Queen Mary* over the years. This particular investigation yielded some very interesting feedback regarding the ghostly population aboard the ship.

The psychic began by stating that there were "spirits all over the ship." In order, she picked up on a John (John Pedder died in 1966); the letters of another name "STAR" (possibly William Stark who died in 1949); a man named Mitchell (possibly Captain G.T. Mitchell [not a captain of the *Queen Mary*] who died in 1967 and was buried at sea); and a man named Charles, who worked on the ship, and may have died on board (Charles Summers died in 1949, on voyage 119, of pancreatitis); the name William, Williams or Bill also came through (W.M. Holden drowned in 1943; William Eric Stark was accidentally poisoned in 1949; William Earnest Humphries died from natural causes in 1950; William Henry Barrett died from a heart attack in 1950; Richard Walter Williams died in 1951; and William Henry Pope died from a prescription overdose in 1964).

Continuing, the psychic also made contact with a lady who wore a long, white dress with dark cuffs, possibly fur-lined, in the salon area of the ship. She stated, "The lady likes the ballroom where she sometimes sings and dances." She also picked up on George Gershwin or Cole Porter music, and the initial "J" (this is in keeping with other stories about a woman with a name beginning with the letter "J"). "The lady may have been an entertainer, who sat by the piano and sang, and loved the ambiance of the ship," the psychic said.

By the pool area, the psychic saw ectoplasm or a fog-like substance and picked up on a woman who may have been pushed into the pool and murdered. In the ballroom, the name Richard or Robert filtered through from the other side (Richard Rolland Metcalf died from a heart attack in 1950; John Robert Maloney died from unknown causes in 1951; and Richard Walter Williams died in 1951).

The psychic investigator stated that some spirits may come to the ship, as if drawn, because they had wonderful times aboard, and they often return to places where they experienced happiness. They represent earth-bound spirits who don't know they have passed on, and continue to repeat the same things they did while alive, going largely unnoticed. Sometimes recognition by another helps them move on; it can be verification that they are dead. When you are near a spirit, it often gets cold, and feels like you are walking through someone. The psychic concluded, "There is so much going on around us that we simply cannot or will not see, but the energy is definitely there. It is nothing to be afraid of. There is no feeling of intent to harm that I can feel on this ship."

A PSYCHIC IN THE NEWS

A recent television special featuring renowned parapsychologist Peter James, provided some startling new information about the paranormal activity on board the ship, as well as further documenting existing phenomena. The extensively researched television segment began with James stating that the *Queen Mary* is purported to have over 600 ghosts aboard the ship. He followed with a confirmation about the numerous sightings, especially in the below-deck areas, and the fact that the ship appears to be "saturated with spiritual energy."

During the segment, stories were related about the "kitchen spirit;" the ghost energy in the pool area; the restless energy where the morgue and coffin storage areas used to be; voices of children crying in the cargo

Children playing in the Nursery

hold area; sounds of footsteps of invisible people running along darkened corridors; ghostly laughter and haunting, unexplained sounds in the Boiler Room; below-deck passageways and abandoned rooms; and the voice of the spirit of a young child, who continues to cry out for her parents (recorded on tape by James).

A SECOND TIME AROUND?

A story with a very unusual twist came by way of a tour guide, who was given this information (on file in the ship's archives) first-hand, and transcribed it as follows: In 1988, the then-Assistant Manager of the

Hotel Queen Mary received a letter from a couple in England. They had sailed on the luxury liner from Southampton to New York in 1958 on their honeymoon, and wanted to celebrate their 30th wedding anniversary on the ship. They requested the same room they had occupied in 1958.

Since the room numbers had changed often over the years, the Assistant Manager had to search the records to see if the room was still in use, and if so, what the number now was. He found the room, and discovered that it was still part of the hotel. He reserved the room and wrote to the couple, assuring them that everything would be as they wished. (He had never met these people, nor spoken to them.)

On the day of the couple's arrival at the ship, the Assistant Manager was behind the front desk of the hotel. They entered the lobby, took one look at him, and froze in their tracks. They would not approach him. They would not speak to him. They would not have anything to do with him. He didn't know what was going on. Had he offended them in some way?

Eventually, the Assistant Manager went into the back office. A few minutes later, the Manager came in and told him to take the next three days off with pay. He offered no explanation. The Assistant Manager left, still not knowing what had happened. He ended up returning from his "vaction" a half-day early because someone had called in sick. He was behind the front desk when the couple came up from "B" Deck to check out. Again, they took one look at him and froze. And again, the Assistant Manager was completely baffled.

After a lengthy period of awkward silence, the woman approached him and began to explain. In 1958, each passenger was usually serviced by one particular steward or stewardess. Instead of giving them a tip every time they brought a drink or a newspaper or whatever, they were often given a chunk of money in a tip envelope at the end of the voyage. This couple had a wonderful steward while on board—great service, great attitude. They wanted to tip him when the *Queen Mary* arrived in New York; however, they couldn't locate him anywhere. He was not on the ship, and no one knew what had happened to him. Eventually, they discovered that the steward had taken ill just before the *Queen Mary* docked, and was taken off the ship to the hospital, where he died.

The couple never saw the Steward again—that is, until they ran into the Assistant Manager—he was the "spitting image" of the Steward.

The resemblance was so uncanny, that the couple was uncomfortable being around him. Even more amazing, is the fact that the Steward died in 1958, *on the same day the Assistant Manager was born!* (The Assistant Manager has since passed away, perhaps finally joining his "spirit double.")

GHOSTS WEREN'T IN HER CONTRACT

Prior to becoming an employee aboard ship, S.J.G. became a **Queen Mary** Ghost Club initiate. Her first encounter with the unknown occurred while completing what she thought was a quick contracting job aboard the ship. This is her story:

Her first encounter began after the current CEO received the lease to operate the **Queen Mary** in 1993. She was contracted to dress the windows in Piccadilly Circus before the Grand Re-opening event being planned. The previous management had closed the ship, and it was not open for business until the second quarter, 1993.

Empty corridor during conversion to a tourist attraction

Security was located in an area that is currently known as Queen's Marketplace, away from the ship. This added to her sense of uneasiness and feeling of isolation. The atmosphere was unique in terms of lighting, sound and temperature. She felt the need to work quickly, get the job done and get out. As she decorated the half-circle windows to the Kodak Shop, the *normal* ambiance seemed to give way to a completely *different* feel. "If one assumed that I was a little frightened, he would be correct," S.J.G. stated. She decided not to look around because she felt that someone was continually watching her, and wasn't particularly keen on finding out who it was. So, she concentrated on the job at hand. All she could think of was finishing her work and getting off the ship.

S.J.G. said, "It seemed as if noises were coming from all around. There was a constant *whooshing* sound as if crowds of people were moving by me. Hammering and banging noises, coming from several decks below, filled the night. At 1:00 a.m. I really wanted to leave the ship, even though I'm not easily frightened. To relieve the tension, and maybe placate whoever or whatever was there, I repeated over and over in my mind, 'I'm here making your ship very attractive, and I'm here to help, so don't hurt or scare me.' I managed to get my work finished, and never did see a ghost, but I certainly felt *something* all the time I was there."

More recently, S.J.G. had another strange encounter. Her office is located on "A" Deck, midship, portside. According to preliminary research, the office used to serve as the loading lobby for passenger luggage in the early years of the ship's operation. In fact, it still retains the sealed doors which once opened to the outside.

The first two months S.J.G. worked there, during the summer of 1995, she noticed the smell of *Old Spice* cologne outside her door near the fire extinguisher. (Her office is nestled between two hotel rooms.) The first time it happened was around 8:00 a.m. "The smell of cologne was so strong, that I assumed it must be a businessman staying in an adjacent room," S.J.G. revealed. However, there was no evidence of anyone occupying the room.

The next occurrence also took place during the morning hours, a few days later. Again, the smell was so strong, that it permeated her office. S.J.G. immediately ran out to see if she could spot someone. Glancing down the corridor, hoping to catch sight of the responsible party, she saw no one. This time she felt that the cologne belonged to an elderly gentleman because the scent was so over-powering. (The sense of smell is one of the first to weaken as people age.)

Two weeks later, after lunch, she was going back to her office, when the smell of *Old Spice* again lingered outside the entrance. I permeated the area, and she looked at the carpet to see if perhaps someone had spilled a bottle of the cologne. She found nothing. The last time this happened, she checked everywhere and was again left without a clue.

S.J.G. told us, "I figured that I may have a gentleman spirit watching over me, so I decided to accept his presence and not question the purpose of his visits. I was curious, however, and decided to have a friend research the date that *Old Spice* was originally marketed. Oddly enough, it turned out that the cologne was first manufactured in 1936, the year of the maiden voyage of the *Queen Mary!*"

SEANCE OF OCTOBER 27, 1987

Debbie Christenson Senate, a psychic, performed a seance aboard the *Queen Mary* on the night of October 27, 1987. She went into a deep trance at approximately 12:06 a.m. Eighteen people were present in a small circle. Several spirits made their presence known during the seance. The following represents an account of the event which is taken directly from *The Haunted Southland* by Richard Senate.

Debbie sat up in her chair, her eyes still closed, her face twisted in pain.

(Debbie): "My legs," she cried out, "My legs, pain."
(Richard): "What is the matter with your legs?"
(Debbie): "Pain. My legs are wounded."
(Richard): "What is your name?"
(Debbie): "Carlo."
(Richard): "Did you have another name?"
(Debbie): "Carlo Giovetti," she answered in a pained voice.
(Richard): "Are you Italian?"
(Debbie): "Si."
(Richard): "How were your legs injured?"
(Debbie): "Shot down, crashed."
(Richard): "Who shot you down?"
(Debbie): "English," She said with a sneer of hate, "English Spitfires."
(Richard): "What year is this?"
(Debbie): "1941."
(Richard): "What did you do?"
(Debbie): "Pilot, Regia Aeronotica."
(Group Member): What kind of plane did you fly?"

(Debbie): Falco, Falco, CR 42 Falco."
(Richard): "What was this plane like?"
(Debbie): Biplane, Falco is a good plane."
(Richard): Biplanes were not used that late. Are you sure it was a biplane, two wings?"
(Debbie): "Si, Falco."
(Richard): "Where were you based?"
(Debbie): "Bengali, Bengali."
(Group Member): Is that in North Africa?"
(Debbie): "Si."
(Richard): "How did you get to North Africa?"
(Debbie): "Kangaroo, I was kangarooed."
(Richard): "What is a Kangaroo? Was that the name of a ship?"
(Debbie): Airplane, Kangaroo. Falco folded up. Placed in Kangaroo. My plane was folded up."
(Richard): "Did you mean your Falco folded up and crashed?"
(Debbie): "No, no, Kangarooed. SM 82, flown to Bengali."
(Richard): "What is a Kangaroo?," I asked for a second time.
(Debbie): "Plane, three-motored transport."
(Group Member): "Your plane was folded up inside another larger plane and flown to North Africa?"
(Debbie): "Si."
(Richard): "What was your squadron number?"
(Debbie): "162-B, no, 162-A."
(Richard): "What were you doing the day you were shot down?"
(Debbie): "Reconnaissance over Bar Dee Ah."
(Richard): "What happened after you were shot down?"
(Debbie): "Captured by British. Taken to Alexandria."
(Richard): "What happened then. Did the British take care of your legs?"
(Debbie): "No. British kicked me. Placed on board the Queen Mary."
(Richard): "Where were you placed?"
(Debbie): "In the bottom of the ship. The air was hot, so hot."
(Richard): Did you see a Doctor?"
(Debbie): "The English want to cut off my legs! I won't let them. Bugs are crawling all over my legs. Make them stop!"
(Richard): "Why do they want to amputate your legs?"
(Debbie): I will never fly again. Don't let them cut off my legs."
(Richard): "What is it like on the ship?"
(Debbie): "Infantry - infantry. They placed me with the infantry men, pigs!"
(Richard): "Where were they taking you?"
(Debbie): "Australia."
(Richard): "Were there any injured men on this ship?"

(Debbie): "Many, five or six died each day. It was so hot."

(Richard): "What did they do with the dead?"

(Debbie): "Overboard."

(Richard): "Was there a priest on board? Someone to confide in, for last rites?"

(Debbie): "No priest. My legs hurt so bad. I can't feel them now. Oh mama! Oh mama!"

(Richard): "What's happening now?"

(Debbie): "They put me in a bag, a canvas bag. It's cold, the water is so cold"."

Debbie let out a scream and fell forward in her chair.

In an effort to substantiate Carlo's story, the research proved quite interesting. Archival information on file at the Imperial War Museum in London revealed that a bomber/transport, referred to as the **SM-82** (Savoia-Marchetti), was first flown in 1938. A three-engine craft, it helped supply the Italian Army in Africa, operating until 1960. The design of the plane enabled a complete **CR42** biplane to be housed, once its wings and tail surfaces were detached and stored longitudinally. At least 50 fighters were transported to Africa in this manner.

Drills during World War II

The *SM-82* was also called *Canguro* (Carlo's Kangaroo), or *Marsupiale.* When Italy entered the war, she possessed 12 of these transport vehicles, forming Squadrons *607a* and *608a* of the *49a Gruppo* at Naples.

Additionally, the *CR42* was the last biplane to be constructed by Fiat, and one of the last biplane fighters built anywhere in the world. The *CR42,* Falco (or Falcon) was first flown in early 1939, and placed in production the same year. Technological advancements in airplanes phased out the use of the Falco in 1945. Finally, the *CR42* served in North Africa, just as Carlo had said.

Other documentation corroborates the fact that voyages during wartime were indeed hellish. They were very tense and emotional. The crew and soldiers were on constant alert for German U-boats who were trying to sink the *Queen Mary*. Fortunately, her speed and evasive tactics at sea, saved her from peril. Aboard ship, the heat was oppressive, especially during the voyages to Australia and Egypt.

The pool area jammed with tiers of folding frame beds during the War

Without air conditioning, the decks below became floating sauna baths. It appears as if many soldiers died of heat exhaustion. Tempers flared, gangs operated below deck and threats of mutiny occurred during these voyages. Frequent salt water showers were the only relief. By November, during the time of the *Queen Mary's* final war-time run from Australia to Suez, they had delivered 80,000 Anzac troops to Egypt, while returning with many Italian prisoners-of-war for confinement in Australia.

It would appear that the story of the painful journey of an Italian prisoner-of-war, one Carlo Giovetti (though the name cannot be verified) a biplane pilot for the Italian Air Force, holds a great deal of credibility. Like John Pedder, William Eric Stark, Miss Turner and Mrs. Kilburn, Carlo has a name; however most remain nameless—for the moment.

The list of encounters appears endless, with stories as numerous as the ghosts who inhabit the ship. People from all walks of life have seen, heard, or felt something in certain areas of the ship—from Shaft Alley to the Bridge.

Ghosts rarely materialize; however, they do leave traces, if you are sensitive, or open enough to believe in the possibility of their existence. Hopefully, you will be one of the lucky few to be given a glimpse of their appearance, a touch indicating their presence, or a whisper of their name.

As a final thought, no one who has been involved in a paranormal event while on the ship has ever expressed a feeling of being threatened, or sensed that they would be harmed in any way. People have stated over and over that a healthy fear of the unknown has been present in most who have had an encounter; this is a natural emotion. In fact, the overall impression from crew and visitors alike, is that the experiences were refreshing, fun and exciting; and the ghosts aboard the ship appear to be friendly.

As one person said, "They are just doing their thing while we do ours. If we happen to enter their world, we should just say 'excuse me,' and move on."

For those wishing to spend more than an afternoon aboard the **Queen Mary** in search of ghostly phenomena, we suggest spending the night in one of the 365 recently restored original First Class staterooms for a unique and wonderful experience that you won't soon forget. While varying in size, decor and view, each room contains the most up-to-date amenities; and if you want to take a break from your ghosthunting activities, there are a number of places to dine. There is also an evening full of entertainment, including dancing, if you're in the mood. To book your stay and enjoy the real spirit of the ship, call (310) 432-6964, or (800) 437-2934, or your travel agent.

Until then... *HAPPY HAUNTING* !

REFERENCES

Abbott, Geoffrey
1986   Ghosts of The Tower of London. David and Charles.

Auerback, Loyd
1986 ESP, Hauntings and Poltergeists. Warner Books, Inc. N.Y.

Bayless, Raymond
1973 Apparitions and Survival of Death. University Books, N.Y.

Bingham, Joan, and Dolores Riccio
1991 More Haunted Houses. Pocket Books. N.Y

Blanchard, Fessenden S.
1960 Ghost Towns of New England. Dodd, Mead and Co., N.Y.

Brooks, J.A.
1982 Ghosts of London. Jarrold Publishing, Norwich, Great Britain.
1990 Britain's Haunted Heritage. Jarrold Publishing, Norwich, Great Britain.

Cahill, Robert Ellis
1983 New England's Ghostly Haunts. Chandler-Smith Publishing House

Cohen, Daniel
1984 The Encyclopedia of Ghosts. Dodd, Mead and Co. N.Y.

Curran, Robert, Jack & Janet Smurl, and Ed and Lorraine Warren
1993 The Haunted. St. Martin's Paperbacks, N.Y.

Fodor, Nandor
1958 On the Trail of the Poltergeist. Citadel Press, N.Y.
1959 The Haunted Mind. New American Library, N.Y.
1968 The Unaccountable. Award Books, N.Y.

Forman, Joan
1987 Haunted Royal Homes. Jarrold Publishing, Norwich, Great Britain.
1989 The Haunted South. Jarrold Publishing, Norwich, Great Britain.

Haining, Peter
1975 Ghosts. Macmillan Publishing Company.

Hippisley-Coxe, A.D.
1973 Haunted Britain. Hutchinson.

Holzer, Hans
1968 Ghosts of the Golden West. The Bobbs-Merrill Co. N.Y.
1969 Window to the Past. Doubleday & Co., Inc. N.Y.
1974 Haunted Hollywood. The Bobbs-Merrill Co. N.Y.
1983 True Ghost Stories. Prentice Hall, Englewood Cliffs. N.J.
1990 Ghosts, Hauntings and Possessions: The Best of Hans Holzer,
      Book 1. Llewellyn Publications, St. Paul, Minnesota.
1992 Ghosts, Hauntings and Possessions: The Best of Hans Holzer,
      Book 2. Llewellyn Publications, St. Paul, Minnesota.

Hopkins, R. Thurston
1953 Ghosts Over England. Meridian Books.
1956 Cavalcade of Ghosts. World's Work.

Inglis, Brian
1985 The Paranormal: An Encyclopedia of Psychic Phenomena. Granada
      Publishing, London.

Jacobson, Laurie, and Marc. Wanamaker
1994 Hollywood Haunted. A Ghostly Tour of Filmland. Angel City Press,
      Santa Monica.

Jarvis, Sharon
1985 True Tales of the Unknown. Bantam Books. N.Y.
1992 Dead Zones. Warner Books, Inc. N.Y.

MacKenzie, Andrew
1970 The Unexplained: Some Strange Cases of Psychical Research.
      Popular Library, N.Y.
1971 Apparitions and Ghosts. Arthur Barker.
1982 Hauntings and Apparitions. Granada Publishing, London.

Maguglin, Robert O.
1993 The Official Pictorial History: The Queen Mary. RMS Foundation,
      Inc., Long Beach, California.

Marinacci, Mike
1988 Mysterious California. Panpipes Press. Los Angeles.

May, Antoinette
1977   Haunted Houses and Wandering Ghosts of California. Examiner
       Special Projects, San Francisco.
1993   Haunted Houses of California. Wide World Publishing. California.

Metcalfe, Leon
1972   Discovering Ghosts. Shire Publications.

Myers, Arthur
1986   The Ghostly Register. Contemporary Books. Chicago.
1990   The Ghostly Gazetteer: America's Most Fascinating Haunted
       Landmarks. Contemporary Books. Chicago.
1993   A Ghosthunter's Guide To Haunted Landmarks, Parks, Churches,
       And Other Public Places. Contemporary Books, Chicago.

Norman, Diana
1977   The Stately Ghosts of England. Dorset Press. N.Y.

O'Donnell, Elliott
1990   Scottish Ghost Stories. Jarrold Publishing, Norwich, Great Britain.

Oppel, Frank
1985   Tales of the New England Coast. Castle, Secaucus, N.J.

Randles, Jenny, and Peter Hough
1993   The Afterlife: An Investigation Into the Mysteries of Life After
       Death. Berkley Books, N.Y.

Rawcliffe, D.H.
n.d.   Occult and Supernatural Phenomena. Dover Publications, N.Y.

Reinstedt, Randall
1974   Ghosts, Bandits and Legends of Old Monterey. Ghost Town
       Publications, Carmel, California.
1977   Ghostly Tales and Mysterious Happennings of Old Monterey.
       Ghost Town Publications, Carmel, California.
1980   Incredible Ghosts of Old Monterey's Hotel Del Monte. Ghost Town
       Publications, Carmel, California.

RMS Foundation, Inc.
n.d.   A Guide to the Upper Decks of the Queen Mary. Long Beach, CA

Rogo, Scott D.
1977 <u>Parapsychology: A Century of Inquiry.</u> Dutton, N.Y.

Scenic Art, Incorporated
1993 <u>R.M.S. Queen Mary Superliner Pictorial.</u> Oakland, California.

Scott, Beth, and Michael Norman
1987 <u>Haunted Heartland.</u> Warner Books. N.Y.

Senate, Richard L.
1985 <u>Ghosts of the Haunted Coast.</u> Pathfinder Publishing. Ventura.
1986 <u>Ghosts of Southern California.</u> Pathfinder Publishing. Ventura.
1991 <u>Haunted Ventura.</u> Charon Press, Ventura, California.
1994 <u>The Haunted Southland</u>. Charon Press, Ventura, California.

Smith, Susy
1967 <u>Prominent American Ghosts.</u> The World Publishing Company. N.Y.
1967 <u>Haunted Houses for the Millions.</u> Bell Publishing Company, N.Y.

Steadman, G., and Ray Anker
1977 <u>Ghosts of the Isle of Wight</u>. I.W. Country Press.

Steiger, Sherry Hansen, and Brad Steiger
1990 <u>Hollywood and the Supernatural.</u> St. Martin's Press.

Underwood, Peter
1973 <u>Haunted London</u>. Harrap.
1984 <u>The Haunted Isle</u>. Harrap.

USA Weekend
1992 <u>I Never Believed In Ghosts Until...: 100 Real-Life Encounters.</u>
Contemporary Books, Chicago.

Warren, Ed and Lorraine, and Robert David Chase
1991 <u>Ghost Hunters.</u> St. Martin's Paperbacks, N.Y.

Webb, Richard
1971 <u>Great Ghosts of the West.</u> Nash, Los Angeles.

A comprehensive catalogue of books on ghosts and hauntings is available through
***Invisible Ink**, 1811 Stone Wood Drive, Beavercreek, Ohio 45432, or call 1-800-31-GHOST.*

SELECTED GHOST MOVIES

Haunted Castle (1921)
One Frightened Night (1935)
Topper Takes A Trip (1939)
The Ghost Comes Home (1940)
Topper Returns (1941)
The Ghost of Frankenstein (1942)
Ghost Ship (1943)
Ghost Catchers (1944)
The Canterville Ghost (1944)
The Time of Their Lives (1946)
Ghost Chasers (1951)
Ghost of Dragstrip Hollow (1959)
Ghosts of Rome (1961)
The Ghost (1963)
Ghost in the Invisible Bikini (1966)
Ghosts Italian Style (1969)
The Legend Of Hell House (1973)
Ghost in the Noonday Sun (1973)
Poor Girl, A Ghost Story (1975)
Cathy's Curse (1976)
The Evil (1978)
The Changling (1979)
The Shining (1980)
House of the Dead (1980)
The Haunting of Julia (1981)
Soul Survivor (1982)
The Keep (1983)
The Entity (1983)
The Haunting Passion (1983)-TV
The Ghost Writer (1984)
House Where Evil Dwells (1985)
The Heavenly Kid (1985)
The Legend of Hell House (1985)
Ghost Fever (1985)
Frenchman's Farm (1986)
Poltergeist II (1986)
Ghostriders (1987)
Made In Heaven (1987)
Angel Heart (1987)

The Ghost Goes West (1935)
Topper (1937)
The Ghost Breakers (1940)
Hold That Ghost (1941)
Here Comes Mr. Jordan (1941)
Ghosts on the Loose (1943)
Between Two Worlds (1944)
The Uninvited (1944)
The Ghost & Mrs. Muir (1946)
Ghosts of Berkeley Square(1947)
House on the Haunted Hill (1958)
13 Ghosts (1960)
Carnival of Souls (1962)
The Haunting (1963)
The Ghost and Mr. Chicken (1966)
The Other (1973)
Don't Look Now (1973)
Madhouse Mansion (1974)
Burnt Offerings (1976)
Heaven Can Wait (1978)-Remake
Inferno (1978)
The Hearse (1980)
Somewhere in Time (1980)
Ghost Story (1981)
Kiss Me Goodbye (1982)
Poltergeist (1982)
Christine (1983)
One Dark Night (1983)
Ghostbusters (1984)
The Oracle (1985)
The Fog (1985)
The Supernaturals (1985)
Maxie (1985)
Nomads (1986)
The Wraith (1986)
The Canterville Ghost (1986)-Remake
Eyes of Fire (1987)
Siesta (1987)
Ghost Fever (1987)

SELECTED GHOST MOVIES - Continued

Poltergeist III (1987)
Sister, Sister (1988)
Gotham (1988)-TV
Lady in White (1988)
Ghostbusters II (1989)
Chances Are (1989)
In The Dead Of Night (1989)-TV
Heart of Midnight (1989)
Field of Dreams (1989)
Flatliners (1990)
Ghost Dad (1990)
Heart Condition (1990)
The Forgotten One (1990)
Jacob's Ladder (1990)
Defending Your Life (1991)
Truly, Madly, Deeply (1992)
Candyman (1992)
Hearts and Souls (1993)
The Crow (1994)
Casper (1995)

Ghost Town (1988)
Beetlejuice (1988)
Wings of Desire (1988)
The Haunting of Sarah Hardy (1989)
Always (1989)
High Spirits (1989)
The Other (1989)
Turn of the Screw (1989)-TV
Ghost (1990)
Ghosts Can't Do It (1990)
The First Power (1990)
In the Spirit (1990)
A Ghost in Monte Carlo (1990)
Dead Again (1991)
Switch (1991)
Death Becomes Her (1992)
The Green Man (1992)
The House of Spirits (1993)
Candyman II (1995)

[DOCUMENTING YOUR OWN EXPERIENCES ABOARD THE QUEEN MARY]

NAME_____.

ADDRESS_____.

CITY_____STATE_____.

ZIP CODE_____-_____.

PHONE (HOME:_____.   OTHER NUMBER: _____.

BIRTH DATE _____.   OCCUPATION_____.

MARRIED_____ SINGLE_____ NO. OF CHILDREN_____.

NO. OF PEOPLE RESIDING AT PLACE OF EVENT:_____.

NO. OF PEOPLE WITNESSING THE EVENT:_____.

NAME OF OTHER PERSON WHO WITNESSED EVENT:
#1_____. RELATIONSHIP_____. AGE ____.
NAME OF OTHER PERSON WHO WITNESSED EVENT:
#2_____. RELATIONSHIP_____. AGE_____.
NAME OF OTHER PERSON WHO WITNESSED EVENT:
#3_____. RELATIONSHIP_____. AGE _____.

OTHER WITNESSES BY NAME AND AGE:

_____
_____.

WERE ANY PETS PRESENT? (if yes, explain):_____
_____.

DATE(S) EVENT(S) OCCURRED:_____
_____.

APPROXIMATE TIME(S) EVENT(S) OCCURRED:_____
_____.

WEATHER CONDITIONS PRESENT:_____
_____.

BRIEFLY DESCRIBE THE EVENT:_____
_____

DESCRIBE YOUR FEELINGS AT THE TIME OF THE EVENT:_____
_____.

IN WHAT ROOM(S) DID/DOES THE EVENT OCCUR?:_____
_____.

DESCRIBE FURNISHINGS IN THE ROOM(S) WHERE THE EVENT(S)
OCCURRED_____.

APPROXIMATE DURATION OF EVENT:_____
_____.

HAVE EVENTS OCCURRED BEFORE? (IF YES, BRIEFLY EXPLAIN):_____
_____.

HAVE THE EVENTS INCREASED IN FREQUENCY? (IF YES, BRIEFLY EXPLAIN):
_____.

DO YOU KNOW THE HISTORY OF THE PLACE? (IF YES, BRIEFLY EXPLAIN):
_____
_____.

DO YOU KNOW THE NAME OF THE PRIOR OWNER(S)?:_____
_____.

IF YOU CAN, DRAW WHAT YOU SAW IN THIS BOX.

Please return this questionnaire to *G-Host Publishing*,
8701 Lava Place, West Hills, CA 91304-2126
or Fax: 818-340-6676

(Thank you for your time and patience in completing this form).

WHAT TO DO IF YOU SEE A
GHOST

(Suggestions to help you cope while continuing to investigate)

1. Don't panic; sit back and enjoy the phenomenon, and try to notice every detail you can.

2. After the event, write down exactly what you saw in as much detail as possible. Remember if there were any particular smells; sensations such as cold spots, gusts of air, or feelings of nausea; music playing or other audible sounds; voices or conversations in the background; or feelings of being watched or touched, etc.

3. Try and sketch what you saw; what the image was wearing, including the style of clothing, shoes, glasses, hats, etc., anything which may give an indication of a particular time period or era.

4. Draw a diagram or map of where the apparition was seen, and where you were when the event took place. Note furniture, windows, or other features in relation to the sighting.

5. Note what time of the day the event took place, as well as weather conditions and temperature, if possible.

6. Record general information regarding how the event made you feel (happy, sad, frightened... etc.).

7. Note any unusual circumstances surrounding the event, including; storms, power outages, other people working in the area, etc.).

8. Note other people present; including any children or animals who might have witnessed the event, or may have been affected.

9. Attempt to investigate the experience further; including who the ghost might have been; attempt to rule out any explainable causes for the occurrence; and try to research the area in more detail.

A GUIDE TO
THE HAUNTED QUEEN MARY

ORDER FORM:

Please send me_____copies of *A Guide To The Haunted Queen Mary*. The purchase price is $9.95 (DO NOT SEND CASH). To order by mail, please add the following:

* For postage and handling in the United States, please add $3.00 for each book, (allow 3-4 weeks for delivery).
* All California residents add $.82 / book to cover sales tax.
* For Foreign orders (including Canada) add $5.00 for postage and handling.
* Contact the Merchandising Department for discounts on multiple orders over 10.
* Charge your order by phone or Fax:

☐ VISA   ☐ MasterCard   ☐ American Express

Card Number _____ Expiration _____

You may also purchase the book on board the Queen Mary, or ask your favorite bookstore to order it for you.

U.S. Orders: $9.95 x no. of copies = $_____
Shipping (U.S.): $3.00 x no. of copies = $_____
Shipping (Foreign): $5.00 x no. of copies = $_____
Sales tax (California only): $.82 x no. of books = $_____
                                       TOTAL ENCLOSED $_____

SEND CHECK OR MONEY ORDER (U.S. FUNDS) TO:

HAUNTED QUEEN MARY
THE QUEEN MARY (Merchandising Department)
1126 Queens Highway, Long Beach, California 90802-6390 USA
PHONE: (310) 435-3511 Extension 5853; or FAX ORDER (310) 437-4531

MAIL MY BOOK(S) TO:

Name:_____
Address:_____
City:_____
State:_____ Zip Code:_____
Phone Number (   ) _____

- Notes -

- Notes -